Better Homes and Gardens®

YOUR
WALLS &
CEILINGS

BETTER HOMES AND GARDENS® BOOKS

Editor: Gerald M. Knox
Art Director: Ernest Shelton
Managing Editor: David A. Kirchner

Associate Art Director (Managing): Randall Yontz
Associate Art Directors (Creative): Linda Ford, Neoma Alt West
Copy and Production Editors: Marsha Jahns, Nancy Nowiszewski,
Lamont Olson, Mary Helen Schiltz, David A. Walsh
Assistant Art Director: Harijs Priekulis
Graphic Designers: Mike Burns, Alisann Dixon, Mike Eagleton,
Lynda Haupert, Deb Miner, Lyne Neymeyer, Trish Church-Podlasek,
Stan Sams, D. Greg Thompson, Darla Whipple, Paul Zimmerman

Editor in Chief: Neil Kuehnl
Group Editorial Services Director: Duane L. Gregg

General Manager: Fred Stines
Director of Publishing: Robert B. Nelson
Director of Retail Marketing: Jamie Martin
Director of Direct Marketing: Arthur Heydendael

All About Your House: Your Walls & Ceilings

Project Editor: James A. Hufnagel
Associate Editors: Walter D. Brownfield, Willa Rosenblatt Speiser
Assistant Editor: Leonore A. Levy
Contributing Senior Writer: Paul Kitzke
Copy and Production Editors: Marsha Jahns, Lamont Olson
Building and Remodeling Editor: Joan McCloskey
Furnishings and Design Editor: Shirley Van Zante
Garden and Outdoor Living Editor: Beverly Garrett
Money Management and Features Editor: Margaret Daly

Art Director: Linda Ford
Graphic Designer: Harijs Priekulis

Contributors: Denise L. Caringer, James Downing, Rose Gilbert,
Cathy Howard, Paul Krantz, Jill Mead, Stephen Mead, Marcia Spires

Special thanks to William Hopkins, Babs Klein, and
Don Wipperman for their valuable contributions to this book.

INTRODUCTION

In *Your Walls & Ceilings*, you'll find just about equal parts of inspiration, information, and practical, step-at-a-time guidance. Here you'll find ways to decorate and improve the walls and ceilings at your house. We'll show you how to plan major improvements, and how to select the materials you'll need for those improvements. But *Your Walls & Ceilings* doesn't stop there. We'll also show—in more than 120 drawings and color photographs—exactly how you can take matters into your own two hands.

Read "When Does it Pay to Do Work Yourself?" on pages 102 and 103 and you'll understand one big reason why we decided to include plenty of step-by-step, how-to information. Typically, the cost of wall and ceiling projects involves a greater proportion of labor to materials than do most other improvements. What's more, a majority of wall and ceiling projects—painting and papering, putting up paneling, even building a new partition—can be mastered by just about anyone. In fact, we've learned that these are the around-the-house jobs most people are likely to do themselves.

This doesn't mean that *Your Walls & Ceilings* is simply another do-it-yourself manual. Like other books in the **ALL ABOUT YOUR HOUSE** series, this volume starts out by showing how to look at your home in a different way, then goes on to tell how you can decorate it, what you can do to make it better, and how you can keep it in top condition. There even are chapters on selecting the art you hang on your walls and upgrading the insulation that goes inside them.

Do be warned, though, that the ideas you'll see here can be infectious. Feel free to borrow and adapt them. You'll find *Your Walls & Ceilings* a valuable resource, and you'll probably want to consider augmenting it with other volumes from the **ALL ABOUT YOUR HOUSE** Library. We believe this unique series of Better Homes and Gardens® books is the most comprehensive encyclopedia of home decorating, improvement, planning, and management ever published.

YOUR WALLS
& CEILINGS

CONTENTS

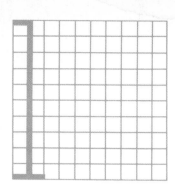

CHAPTER 1

BEGIN WITH A SURVEY OF YOUR HOME'S SURFACES

Because they're all around us most of the time, it's easy to forget the role walls and ceilings play in our environment. They shape our rooms, influence our moods, define interior spaces, and shelter us from the outside world. This introductory chapter encourages you to take an analytical look at the wall and ceiling surfaces at your house and determine whether they're doing their best for your family.

BORED WITH BASIC WHITE?

Sometimes the best thing to do with a room's "envelope" is to paint it white and forget it. White wall and ceiling surfaces virtually fade away, so if you want to make a space look bigger or play up its contents, paint it white.

If, on the other hand, you're growing tired of living in bland, white rooms, consider some alternatives.

The power of paint

One of the quickest, easiest, and thriftiest ways to perk up your rooms and add almost instant personality is with a fresh coat of paint. Here, for example, burnt orange walls add decorative impact to an ordinary room. Without the warm color (complemented by lush, forest green upholstery), this room might look like any other plain white box.

Of course, choosing colors calls for courage, and confidence that your selection will work out the way you intend it to. Chapter 2—New Looks from a Can or by the Roll —presents the basic decorating principles to keep in mind, along with more examples of what paint can do for a room. If you need to brush up on basic painting techniques, that chapter also tells what you need to know about choosing and applying today's finishes.

Other treatments

Paint isn't the only way to achieve an other-than-white room. Wall coverings offer a popular alternative. Chapter 2 also tells how to select and work with this versatile decorating tool. And then there are more durable treatments such as paneling, mirrors, metal, brick, and tile. Chapter 3—Easy-Care Surfaces—explains what you need to know about these materials.

HOW'S THE LIGHT?

What you choose to do with the walls and ceilings at your house depends to a surprising extent on the amount and quality of light they are exposed to. Dimly lit zones demand different treatments than areas that are bathed in sunlight. Cool, north-facing spaces don't behave, in a visual sense, the same as rooms that look to the south. Before you zero in on a particular wall or ceiling treatment, make sure you're looking at your home's surfaces in the proper light.

Bright sunlight keynotes the airy living room shown here. To play up the sunny look, the owners painted walls and ceilings a warm white. Exposed ceiling beams add just the right touch of woody, textural contrast to the painted walls. Finally, the white walls and ceilings also help reflect maximum light, especially important in a room in which an impressive array of plants is grown.

When you're considering colors other than white, remember these guidelines: Bright, intense colors will add warmth to north-facing rooms that get precious little sunlight. Bright colors can also add coziness by visually making the walls and ceilings advance into the room. On the other hand, cool colors, such as blues and greens, can cool down a south-facing room subjected to too much sunlight.

Or you can cut glare with dark colors. They absorb much of the light that strikes them. Rough textures also can have a light-reducing effect. This doesn't mean you can't use dark brown paint, for example, or rough-sawn paneling in a small room, but you should understand how the treatment will affect the room's mood and light level. If a dark color or a woody texture is your choice, you may want to plan additional artificial lighting to compensate. An extra table lamp, a brighter bulb, an uplight tucked into a dark corner, or perimeter lighting built into a cornice or a valance are just a few ways to add light.

Let the walls come down
If you're really determined to brighten a room, consider moving or removing a wall or two, or opening up the ceiling.

Rooms that reach for the roofline, as this one does, appear bigger and lighter than they are. Maybe a simple structural change could do wonders for a room at your house.

Of course, the trouble and expense of any remodeling project dictate that you carefully think through all the consequences before you begin. Chapter 6—Planning Wall and Ceiling Changes—shows a few drafting tricks that can help you to precisely work out your ideas on paper first. With a good set of plans in hand, you then need to decide who will do the work. Does it make sense to take on a wall or ceiling project yourself, or are you better off hiring a contractor? The final pages of Chapter 6 can help you decide.

Then turn to Chapter 7—Building New Walls and Ceilings—and you'll see, one step at a time, how drywall partitions, acoustic tile, and suspended ceilings take shape. More than 50 color photographs guide you through every stage of the construction process.

Finally, keeping a room's surfaces clean and in good repair goes a long way toward brightening its mood (and yours). Chapter 10—Caring for Walls and Ceilings—tells how you can minimize maintenance problems.

ARE THERE ELEMENTS TO PLAY UP—OR DOWN?

How's the architecture at your house? Interesting moldings, fireplaces, window and door details, ceiling angles, and other built-in features give a room character you can capitalize on. Of course, not all architecture is worth emphasizing. Some elements—odd jogs in an attic ceiling, for instance, or a poorly proportioned doorway—deserve to do a disappearing act. And if a *lack* of architectural appeal has you up against a blank wall or ceiling, deft decorating can help you create visual excitement.

Scan the surfaces at your house with a sharp eye for details. Handsome plasterwork, wood paneling or trim, elegant window frames, ceiling cornices, and other embellishments could be hiding under lumpy layers of paint, begging to be rediscovered.

Careful craftsmanship blessed the room at *left* with an authentically colonial character. To highlight the special millwork, the owners chose Williamsburg blue paint and brought wainscoting, fireplace, and window trim to the fore. Deep brown paint emphasizes the molding around the ceiling.

To make certain that other elements don't compete with this architectural detailing, the owners kept the background simple. Creamy white walls and a mellow earth tone on the ceiling give the tall room a cozy feeling.

As you survey your walls and ceilings, look for any elements that make a space special. Here are some of the main possibilities and where in this book you can learn more about exploiting them.

● *Windows.* Curtains or draperies could be masking a room's most outstanding assets. Pages 8, 9, 91, and 94 show dramatic examples of what can happen when windows are played up. If you'd like to "fake" a window where none now exists, turn to pages 36 and 37.

● *Fireplaces.* Nothing provides a cheerier focal point in a room than a good-looking fireplace. If you have one, flaunt it with a special treatment like the mantel restylings shown on pages 12-15. Or add textural interest by exposing a brick fireplace wall, as explained on pages 64 and 65.

● *Ceilings.* Chapter 5—Make Your Ceilings Special—presents ways that paint, paper and fabric, beams, pressed metal, skylights, track lighting, and hanging gardens can give your rooms a lift. Or borrow a trick from Victorian decorators and play up a ceiling by stenciling a frieze around its perimeter. Pages 38 and 39 tell how to work with this almost-forgotten medium.

● *Doors.* Handsome panel doors, even featureless flush doors painted in appealing colors, bring architectural character to otherwise dull rooms. You may even want to go all out and play up doors and doorways with a bold graphic treatment like the one shown on page 35.

Downplaying defects

If contrasting paint or textures can play up a room's assets, then the opposite is true about features you'd like to de-emphasize. For example, to play down the odd angles of an attic ceiling, cover walls and ceilings with the same small overall pattern. Or, if an architectural feature seems to intrude too much into your room, paint or cover it with the same materials as your walls; it will fade into the background.

And in a room with less than perfect proportions, bear in mind that wall and ceiling treatments can visually compensate for awkward dimensions. For example, you can "square up" the proportions in a long, narrow room by painting one or both of the narrow end walls an intense color. If, on the other hand, your room seems too square or boxy, minimize that feeling by using a dramatic wall covering, a mirror, or an eye-catching color on one wall. More about these ploys in Chapter 2—New Looks from a Can or by the Roll.

WHAT'S THE CONDITION OF YOUR WALLS AND CEILINGS?

If your home isn't brand new, your walls and ceilings may have seen better days. Assessing their condition is the first step in any improvement plan. Plaster and drywall develop cracks, wall coverings may blister and peel, and even heavy-duty wood paneling can suffer damage. No matter which decorating option you choose, some prep work will be needed. In Chapter 10—Caring for Walls and Ceilings—you'll learn how to repair walls and ceilings and bring them back to mint condition, or select a wall treatment that will cover up their imperfections.

The success of any surface treatment depends on what's underneath it. Preparing walls and ceilings is the least glamorous part of a makeover, but an absolutely necessary one. How much repair work you'll have to do depends on the condition of your walls and ceilings and the decorating treatment you select.

You'll first want to make sure that your walls and ceilings are structurally sound. Indoor dampness will keep paint and wall covering from adhering properly, and may be warning you of serious leaks that can undermine your home's foundation. Chapter 10 describes how to pinpoint the cause of water seepage and correct it. You'll also find step-by-step instructions for repairing plaster, drywall, wood paneling, and ceramic tile.

If your choice is paint or wall covering, you'll need to make sure that the surface it is going to cover is smooth and grease- and blemish-free. Chapter 2 tells how to prepare and prime walls and ceilings, so that a fresh coat of paint or new wall covering showcases your room instead of spotlighting its bumps, cracks, and imperfections. You'll also find a survey of types of paints and wall coverings that will help you choose one that's suitable for the particular surfaces you plan to cover.

Coverups

If surface damage is severe, you can choose from a variety of wall and ceiling treatments that camouflage defects.

Problem walls can literally be put under wraps. Fabric suspended from rods or stapled over batting (page 84 and cover) soft-pedals less-than-perfect walls. You can add novelty and texture with cover-ups like the straw matting shown on page 31, or the woven hemp panels in the warm living room at *right*. Carpet run up the walls is another cozy and quieting choice.

Wood paneling offers another popular way to cover badly blemished walls. Pages 48-51 and 54 and 55 can help you decide whether you prefer to go with manufactured paneling or solid boards; pages 56-61 tell how to install each type.

Hard choices

Other pages in Chapter 3 present an array of other easy-care surfaces that are as hard-wearing as they are good-looking. Surveyed are traditional favorites such as stone and brick, as well as some unusual options: ceramic tile, mirrors, and metal. You can even bring the look of the outdoors into your home with exterior building materials such as the authentic old barn boards and shakes shown on pages 52 and 53.

If a damaged ceiling or unsightly exposed pipes and ductwork are keeping you from enjoying a room in your home, Chapter 7 shows how to install a new suspended tile ceiling, or opt for pressed metal (pages 88 and 89), an old-time material that's enjoying a renaissance.

WHAT SORT OF MOOD DO YOU WANT TO CREATE?

Whether you want a room to radiate warm, country charm or cool, sophisticated elegance—or something in between—you can achieve it by using color and texture on walls and ceilings. Creating the mood you want in a room can be as simple as changing a wall color or covering. In Chapter 2—New Looks from a Can or by the Roll —you'll learn how to use color and texture to achieve style and unity in a room, and even to redefine a room's size and shape.

In the room at *left*, a pair of raspberry sofas commands center stage, yet it's the color and texture of the walls that set the intimate mood. Far from a bland backdrop, walls like these (covered in gray vinyl) provide shiny contrast to the matte upholstery and nubby rug. The gray walls also pick up blue-gray colors in the rug, helping to balance and emphasize the strong sofa color. (Pages 44 and 45 tell how to select the wall covering that's right for a room; pages 46 and 47, how to put it up.)

In a large room, a deep tone can push walls inward, adding an inviting feeling of coziness. And lavishing your walls and ceilings with white or light-color paint will help open up small rooms.

Divide or merge spaces

Have you considered using wall treatments to define and visually separate different areas in your home? In a newer, open-plan home, for example, you can visually separate adjacent living and dining spots by giving each area a slightly different wall treatment. Mixing colors and patterns within the same space can be tricky. But now you can do just that— without clashing mistakes— with new wall covering and fabric collections. These collections offer you a controlled range of choices for clash-free mixing and matching of colors and patterns. Pages 24 and 25 show an especially appealing example of a coordinated approach.

On the other hand, if you have any cut-up spaces that you want to unify into a cohesive whole, use matching or closely related colors from room to room.

In terms of style, wall and ceiling coverups can work wonders, too, to help you achieve the mood you want. Create the ambience of an old English pub with rough stuccoed walls and wooden beams, for example (pages 86 and 87). Or, add the charm of a bucolic cottage with a country-garden floral print wallpaper. You can add up-to-date crispness to an older home with a modern painted graphic or grid-pattern wall covering, for example (pages 34 and 35), or suggest the elegance of a colonial manor house by adding a colonial-inspired print or stencil to your walls (pages 38 and 39).

Add character

Even if your home has no particular architectural character, don't despair. You can "fake it" by adding "instant architecture" with new moldings from the lumberyard. Even a simple chair rail around the perimeter of a room can add old-fashioned charm. Or, you can nail up intricate new moldings around a ceiling and paint or stain them a contrasting color for emphasis to add decades-old character to a modern-day space.

If your home gets its mood from other factors you want to emphasize (such as a wonderful view or a collection of artwork), the effect you seek to create with your walls and ceilings may be one of understated simplicity so your walls and ceilings slip quietly into the background.

ARE YOU NEGLECTING THE "FORGOTTEN WALLS"?

Look up for a moment. Have you been ignoring your "forgotten walls," the ceilings? Although "basic white" often is a good choice for ceilings, it's not your only alternative. Far from a forgotten surface, your ceilings can be called on to play an important decorative role in your home. They can add dramatic impact as well as change the proportions of a room. You might "raise the roof" visually by painting the ceiling a lighter color than the walls, or do it in actual fact by demolishing the existing ceiling to expose beams and structural supports. Whatever effect you're aiming for, you'll find a variety of decorating options to help you achieve it.

Take a look at the room at *right.* While such a bold graphic is not for everyone, it can add decorative punch—and fun—to an otherwise ho-hum space. In this case, the snappy room scheme centers on a gargantuan pencil graphic that arcs from ceiling to wall. Besides adding color and humor, the mega-pencil softens the boxiness of the room by adding curvilinear emphasis. Pages 34 and 35 tell how to create original graphic treatments. For a subtler painted motif, try a stenciled ceiling border. You'll learn how on page 38.

If you'd like to have a ceiling play more than a supporting role, page through Chapter 5—Make Your Ceilings Special. Here you'll find many variations on the options listed below.

• *Wood* works as well on ceilings as it does on floors. In older homes with attractive woodwork, you can expose existing beams or add false ones to give old-fashioned charm to a contemporary space (pages 86 and 87 explain what's involved in subtracting a ceiling or adding beams). Another interesting choice is wooden lattice. Hung with trailing plants, it can give any room the feeling of an outdoor arbor. Page 121 shows how to build a ceiling trellis.

• *Wall covering* need not stop at the ceiling line. Consider a wallpaper canopy over a bed, or accent an unusually angled ceiling with mini-print wall covering. Lower a too-high ceiling with softly draped fabric, or raise a low ceiling with shiny vinyl or reflective Mylar wall covering. Or double your room's visual space with a mirrored ceiling.

• *Pressed metal,* a turn-of-the-century favorite, is still at home in modern houses. Left bare and gleaming, it's a perfect finishing touch for a high tech kitchen; painted, it complements country furnishings. Pages 88 and 89 tell about pressed metal ceilings.

• *A skylight* (pages 90 and 91) can brighten any room with access to the roof. Impressive as they look, skylights come in kit form and can be installed by a reasonably handy homeowner. Or light up a room with ceiling-mounted track lighting, as explained on pages 92 and 93.

• *Acoustic tiles.* Long for some peace and quiet at home? Contain noise by installing an acoustic tile ceiling in a children's playroom—or any other noisy zone. Chapter 7—How To Build New Walls and Ceilings—tells you how to do it. Ceiling tiles are handy, too, as coverups for damaged surfaces. They can be glued on with a mastic or stapled to furring strips that have been nailed in rows at right angles to the ceiling joists. And today's ceiling tiles offer patterns that simulate wood or elegant old plaster designs.

Shaping space

Varying ceiling heights or treatments is an effective way to define spaces for different activities. A warm ceiling color adds coziness to seating nooks or dining spots. Or use a deeper ceiling color over a dining area or study alcove in an open-plan room. Keep the original low ceiling in the eating section of a living/dining room combination, but let the ceiling soar to spacious new heights in the living room area.

IS ART GETTING TOP DISPLAY?

Have you gotten the hang of choosing and displaying art in your home? Adding a new work of art or rearranging art you already own is one of the quickest ways to revitalize a tired space. If confusion, or lack of expertise about art, has kept you out of the buyer's market, you'll find the terminology demystified in Chapter 4—Express Yourself with Art—so you can confidently choose an intaglio, lithograph, or other original work. And once you've made your selection, you'll learn how to frame and protect it, and how to display it to its—and your room's—best advantage.

You might hesitate before painting your living room bright red, but when it comes to choosing art, you can safely be a bit daring. Because art can be easily moved, rearranged, or replaced, feel free to experiment. Budget-priced posters and reproductions can be welcome additions in themselves, and also can be an inexpensive way to try out ideas and preview their effect before investing in more costly works of art.

If you'd like to purchase an original artwork, you'll have many choices. Oil paintings and acrylics are the most expensive, because the materials themselves are costly, and the artist spends a great deal of time creating each one. An original oil by a well-known artist is likely to be out of your price range, but one painted by a less-famous local artist may fit your budget and give you just as much pleasure.

Works done on paper instead of canvas, such as watercolors, charcoal drawings, and pastels are much more affordable, and their "lightness" compared to oils may be just what you want for a particular room.

Prints

A limited-edition print is another choice. Printmaking is a fine-art form, not to be confused with the mass production of posters or paper reproductions of paintings. Pages 74 and 75 explain the differences, describe various processes used to make prints, and tell you what to look for when buying each type. Silk-screened serigraphs and acid-etched intaglios can become part of your vocabulary, and perhaps part of your home art collection as well.

Frames

Once you've made your purchase, you'll want to frame it properly. Framing protects your artwork from damage, such as warping, fading, and peeling. The right frame also will enhance the appearance of the artwork and complement the decor of the room it's hung in. Unsure whether to cover your artwork with glass or acrylic? Did you know that using anything but acid-free materials in matting and mounting can ruin art done on paper? Do you know how to change the impact of an artwork with a different frame and mat? Pages 76 and 77 will answer your questions about framing.

Hanging art

In the photo at *left*, what could have been a forgotten landing now is a decorative asset thanks to an assemblage of colorful posters and other artwork. Groupings, like the one shown, are a good way to make use of several smaller items or take advantage of a particularly large wall space. In this case, the artworks are tied together by subject matter. You can also group pieces that share colors, or unify disparate items with matching frames and mats. You'll find other guidelines for displaying art on page 79.

Finally, you'll want to enhance your artworks with the right kind of lighting. Whether you choose track lights, uplights, or ones that clamp on to a frame, the information on page 80 will show you how to spotlight your art safely and effectively.

WHAT MORE COULD YOUR WALLS AND CEILINGS DO?

Floor space is not the only usable part of a room. Walls, unused headroom, and even spaces between wall studs can be converted to useful storage. If your rooms are already filled with furniture, but your home still lacks convenient places for everything, look to your walls and ceilings. Here are some of the possibilities.

In the living room at *right*, the beamed ceiling is practical as well as decoratively dramatic. Neither floor nor table space is taken up by lamps; recessed spotlights are fitted right into the beams. Painted a deep aubergine to match an adjoining room, the ceiling has a criss-cross pattern of beams set off with gold-painted stripes that match the walls. The window wall in this room is a hard worker, too. It's been fitted with a long, narrow shelf that holds art objects and plants. Because it runs behind the seating modules, it also does double duty as a handy surface for reading materials or drinks.

Another interesting way to combine a beamed effect with lighting in a room is to install new beams around the perimeter of a room or at one or two ends. Then add fluorescent tubes or incandescent strip lights behind the new beams to wash the walls with light.

Space savers

In the children's room, *opposite*, floor space has been maximized by having both beds and storage anchored to the walls. The storage unit consists of a series of plywood boxes fitted with shelves and doors, a larger unit with a drop-lid work surface, and a closed cabinet.

Need a place to store books and stereo equipment? Or perhaps a specially designed shelving unit for the home

canner? On pages 122-125 you'll find these and other wall storage projects to build.

Uncover hidden assets
The space between wall studs can become a convenient place to store many small items. On pages 126 and 127 you'll learn how to build a recessed pantry and bathroom storage unit.

If you're not a home carpenter, you can purchase many kinds of space-extending wall units. Beds, desks, and dining tables can all fold up "Murphy style" into wall-hung units.

The ideal storage space for infrequently used items may be right above your head. "Dead space" below a hallway or basement ceiling can be fitted with shelves to hold such items as luggage, party supplies, or Christmas decorations. On pages 118 and 119 are instructions for building a workshop catchall and a ceiling-hung storage box.

All the storage ideas mentioned above are discussed in detail in Chapter 8—Put Your Walls and Ceilings to Work—along with the proper way to hang objects on a wall or from a ceiling.

HOW CAN YOUR WALLS AND CEILINGS HELP SAVE ENERGY?

When it comes to the battle against high energy costs, your walls and ceilings constitute the front line of defense—and adequate insulation is one of your best weapons. Poorly insulated attics, basements, and exterior walls lose heat in winter and gain it in summer. The right amount and type of insulation can pay for itself in lower utility bills. And if *your* energy is being sapped by too much household noise, you'll learn in Chapter 9—Insulating and Soundproofing—how to soundproof your rooms.

Any investment in insulation reduces utility bills, but how long will it be before those savings pay for the cost of insulating? Consult the table on page 133 and you can estimate payback periods for your home and climate. Once you've determined your most economy-wise priorities, you'll learn in Chapter 9—Insulating and Soundproofing —how to put them to work.
• *Start at the top.* Warm air rises. An inadequately insulated attic will let your expensively heated air go right through the roof, and take your utility bills with it. Beefing up attic insulation is often your best energy-conservation bet. Whether you do the work yourself or contract it out, pages 136 and 137 tell how to get the job done right. And if you don't have an attic, pages 116 and 117 tell how to insulate an integral ceiling and roof deck such as you might have in a room with a cathedral ceiling.
• *Insulate windows.* The rate at which a surface conserves heat is its R value, and the higher this is, the better. Recommended minimum R values for ceilings and walls are typically double-digit numbers. With windows it's a different story: an uncovered, single-glazed window has an R value of only 0.88. A double-glazed window, at 1.72, isn't much better, and triple-glazing brings the R value up to only 2.56. Clearly, windows—and especially sliding glass doors—are big energy-wasters.

The photo at *right* illustrates an effective way to add insulation to a big expanse of glass. These panels are made from 1-inch rigid foam framed by 1-inch wood edge strips, and covered with skins of ¼-inch hardboard. On the ends of the

panels are 1½x2-inch trim pieces that overlap so their weather-stripped edges seal tightly when the two middle panels are closed.

This treatment illustrates some important points about insulating your windows. To make a window treatment energy-saving, you must provide four things: insulation; a moisture barrier (or sealed edges in the sliding panels) to prevent condensation from forming between the windows and the window covering ; a white or reflective surface facing outside; and edge seals. The most important are the edge seals, which cut down condensation and prevent costly heated air from escaping around the edges.
• *Down under.* An uninsulated basement or crawl space all but puts a house on ice. Insulation not only keeps heated air from escaping from the floor above, but also turns once-cold space into a well-sealed chamber of warm air that serves as a buffer between living space and the chill outside. To learn about insulating these areas, see pages 138 and 139.
• *Exterior walls.* You may be surprised to learn that unless your exterior walls have no insulation whatsoever, adding more is often one of the least cost-effective ways to insulate a home. Pages 40 and 41 explain why, and tell what's involved if you do decide to insulate existing walls.
• *Reducing noise.* If you'd like more peace and quiet as well as more warmth, turn to pages 142 and 143 for some sound suggestions.

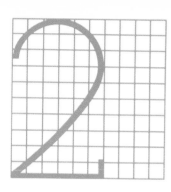

NEW LOOKS FROM A CAN OR BY THE ROLL

Walls can—indeed should—do a lot more than just hold up the ceiling. They are the largest expanses of decorative surfaces you have to work with, and they set the stage for the rest of your furnishings. What you do with your walls can make up for architectural shortcomings, so don't treat them lightly. Do treat them warmly, coolly, quietly, lively, cleverly. Whatever the mood you want to achieve and whatever the room problems you need to overcome, you'll find a universe of possibilities in a can of paint or a few rolls of wall covering.

Color and pattern are two of the most powerful forces in the visual world. Harness them and you can move walls, raise or lower ceilings, stretch floor space, and entirely reshape your home environment.

Fortunately, you don't need a degree in physics (or art) to put the energy of color and pattern to work. In fact, to expand a room, you need to apply only one basic principle: Light colors and unbroken expanses of small patterns make space look larger. This is true because unless an object calls attention to itself, it recedes in your mind. When you are not conscious of a wall, space "feels" more expansive.

The small bedroom at *right* is a case in point. Wrapped entirely in the same mini-pattern print on a light background, it conveys a sense of spaciousness. Wall covering manufacturers help by including matching fabrics in their collections.

When you shop, check out coordinates. Along with fabrics you can sew yourself, you can order ready-made comforters, table linens, window shades, curtains, even accessories.

The same principle applies to paint. One light color over walls, ceiling, and woodwork can do wonders for a small room, especially if you choose window dressing and furniture fabrics that go along with the light color scheme.

CHANGE A ROOM'S DIMENSIONS

Seeing is believing. If you make the most of that maxim, you can "remodel" many problem rooms without ever reaching for a hammer. Paint and wall coverings will do the work for you. Begin by sizing up your room's space. If its dimensions aren't pleasing, you can fool the eye into believing that they are closer to ideal. Reshape your room by emphasizing or eliminating contrast. Use bold, bright colors selectively to draw in a wall or lower a ceiling. Or avoid contrast and let walls and ceilings fade quietly into the background.

Color and contrast are prime factors in our perception of space. If the walls and ceilings of a small room are closing in on you, blur their restrictive boundaries by painting both the same color. To reshape a room that is too long or cavernous, paint end walls or the ceiling a contrasting color to help define the space.

When we go to the movies, the darkened theater seems to disappear as our eyes are drawn to the bright screen. In the small yet dramatic apartment living room *opposite*, the deep forest green surfaces re-

cede, letting light from the windows act like a spotlight. Painting walls and ceilings the same color eliminates their borders, visually expanding the space. The dark surfaces that frame the windows draw attention outside. Vertical blinds seem to enlarge the windows and lift the ceiling even higher, aiding the illusion. To keep the room from appearing too cave-like, a bright yellow rug and sofa catch light from the window and reflect it into the room.

The long and narrow dimensions of the living room *above* once caused a decorating dilemma. Built-in bookcases on one of the longer walls were a focal point. They caught the eye and emphasized the room's length. The room's awkward proportions were "squared up" by painting the end walls a contrasting yellow that pulls them in. The two long walls and the ceiling were painted bright white to visually push them out and give the room an airy, spacious feeling. The once-conspicuous bookcases, now also white, blend into the wall.

27

EMPHASIZE ODDITIES—OR CAMOUFLAGE THEM

Paint and wall coverings can dramatize a room's architectural features or all but obliterate them. Do you want to accent the quirky charm of angles, woodwork, or windows? Then showcase them with deliberate contrast. Perhaps you'd like to downplay aspects of your walls and ceilings that you're not proud of. If so, unify them with a single color or overall pattern. Heavier wall coverings can even hide minor bumps or cracks. Evaluate your room's assets and liabilities, then play them up (or down) for what they're worth.

With so much bland, boxy architecture in houses today, an attic room with interesting ceiling angles might be a blessing you shouldn't disguise. That's what the owners of the room shown here decided to do. Instead of painting or papering nooks and crannies into obscurity, they accentuated them to make a small, under-the-eaves space into a highly individual bedroom.

The problem was a low ceiling and irregular walls. The solution: strong contrast that makes the most of the room's many angles. A wall covering with a small pattern and vertical lines makes the short side walls appear taller. On the ceiling and walls that form the bed alcove, a cream color opens and lightens the space, lifting the claustrophobic feeling of low-ceiling attics. Strong contrast between plain painted surfaces and the patterned wall covering accentuate the room's offbeat proportions. Deep red, repeated in the wall covering and painted into the window-seat alcove, contrasts with the creamy hue to further highlight the ceiling angles.

When decorating a room like the one pictured here, keep in mind that a fine line separates contrast from clash. Don't go overboard with too many colors and patterns in a confined space.

To achieve the opposite effect, minimize architectural oddities by avoiding contrast completely. Nooks, crannies, radiators, and pipes will seem to disappear if you paint them the same solid color as the background. Or you can run the same wall covering up walls and onto ceilings so undesirable corners and angles blend into the walls.

ADD TEXTURE

If you're a good cook, you already understand the importance of varying the textures of the foods you prepare for a meal. The same holds true for your visual diet. Texture, whether it's slick or dull, smooth or rough, gives a room surface appeal and decorative interest. Contrasting textures engage your tactile sense as well as your visual sense. Playing strong textures against subtle ones creates variety in rooms dominated by one color or by a neutral color scheme. In fact, it enriches any decor. Textured wall treatments offer another advantage, especially if you're working with an old house: They can mask a multitude of minor surface blemishes.

In colonial homes, interior walls were left naturally rough. They were nothing more than the unadorned back view of the exterior wall.

Eventually, a smooth coat of plaster was added as a finishing touch for refined householders. Today, we've come full circle: Many of us chip off plaster to get back to the rough textures of brick and stone. The popularity of the country look has also brought back rough-sawn paneling, weathered barn boards, and the good looks of stucco applied with a vigorous trowel.

Texture from a can
In the family room at *right*, a stucco-like finish was created with a premixed acrylic wall coating applied with a putty knife, spread with a trowel, then stroked with a whisk broom. The paint stays pliant long enough for you to work it into the desired pattern and correct any mistakes. Feel free to use your imagination and experiment with combing, stippling with crushed paper towels, or working the coating with your fingertips.

You can get a subtler texture with sand paint, which is available either premixed or with a separate sand powder to stir in. Sand paint is especially effective on ceilings, and it can mask imperfect joints in drywall surfaces.

The fireplace at *right* provides an example of another rough texture—brick veneer. The "bricks," which are actually sliver-thin, are buttered with mortar and pressed in place. (More about brick veneer on pages 66 and 67.)

A gleaming mirror, chrome chairs, and a smooth, wood-topped table balance the rough surfaces in the room. With texture, as with any strong decorating element,

too much of a good thing can be overpowering.

Texture by the roll
Wall coverings also bring texture to a room. You can choose from a wide variety of materials and finishes—silk, linen, grass cloth, and burlap, to name a few. For ultra-posh decorating, you can also buy authentic cowhide and suede, although both are expensive. More economical are embossed vinyl wall coverings, which simulate various natural materials.

If you can squeeze a staple gun, you're on your way to a richly textured wall like the one in the airy bedroom *opposite*. Rush matting, which comes in 4x8-foot sheets and usually spends its life on the floor, wraps the room in a South Seas mood. You can cut these mats with heavy shears and staple them to a wall. Start in a corner, butt and staple at the top, down the joints, and across the bottom. This wall's crisscross motif is reinforced with green cloth tape latticed on a white window shade.

DEVELOP ARCHITECTURAL INTEREST

Until recently, interior architectural details were becoming an endangered species. Soaring building costs, a declining interest in craftsmanship, and changing fashions had all but stamped out the built-in embellishments our grandparents relished. If you miss them, first take a look around. In an older home, you may spot built-in details that have been painted out of sight. If your modern room is devoid of decorative architectural interest, you don't have to be a carpenter to change it. Instead of constructing them, brush on or unroll those missing details.

Think of moldings around wall panels, doors, and windows as *frames,* and paint them to contrast with what they enclose. Three colors provide the impact that updates the bedroom *opposite.* Deep burgundy paint frames wall panels that are painted soft rose and set off with crisp white moldings and ceiling.

The success of a multicolored paint job depends on absolutely straight lines and sharp edges between colors. Where there's a narrow crack, such as between window frames and walls, use a triangular paint shield. Press its edge into the crack so it covers the area you want to protect. Paint, holding the shield in place with one hand and the brush with the other. Wipe the shield often to avoid smears.

Where ceilings meet walls, there are two alternatives. One approach is to use masking tape to ensure clean edges. Unroll and stick tape to the wall a little at a time to avoid stretching and wrinkling it. To prevent seepage and ragged edges, press tape securely to the surface by running your thumb or the bowl of a spoon along the edge of the tape. Remove the tape slowly as soon as paint is dry to the touch. Don't wait until the paint is hard or you'll risk pulling off paint along with the tape.

You can also get straight edges without using tape. Start with a trim brush with a chiseled edge. Hold it firmly by the ferrule with the thumb on one side and the rest of your fingers on the other. Press the brush against the surface until

paint rises to the bristle tips. With a smooth stroke spread this bead of paint along a line $\frac{1}{16}$ of an inch from the edge of the surface you're painting. The paint will spread until it touches the edge.

If your room lacks authentic architectural details, you can create them. In the dining room corner *above,* the dado is painted on and topped with a "chair rail" of wide grosgrain ribbons, overlapped slightly and glued to the wall. Use a level as a ruler to draw straight lines on your wall before applying ribbon. To paint the dado, use masking tape as described earlier.

A strip of wall covering hung horizontally can also take the place of a painted border, or you can frame a panel of wall covering with painted molding.

CREATE BOLD GRAPHICS

Wall and ceiling graphics, which are bold, flat designs worked in paint, tape, or cutouts, give any room a charge of individuality. Use graphics to enliven dead wall space, to accent architectural details, or to divert attention from unwanted features. Your creative efforts will pay off with dramatic effects that are easy on your budget. Best of all, you don't need artistic talent or training. If you can cut, paint, or tape a straight line, you're off to a good start.

Effective graphics begin with a carefully thought-out plan. One way to achieve a professional-looking result is to work out your design to scale on graph paper, using felt markers to simulate the colors. Then enlarge the grid and transfer the design (see page 38 for details on this process). Another approach is to draw your design, take a slide photograph of it, and project it onto the wall or ceiling. With this method you can adjust the size, preview the impact, and adjust your plan right on the wall or ceiling. Once you're satisfied, trace the design onto the wall or ceiling.

Bold straight lines work best for the novice graphic artist.

You can paint single lines using masking tape, as described on page 32. If you'd like more than one narrow parallel line, use a special tape, designed for painting stripes on cars. This tape is an inch wide and is scored with strips that can be pulled out to expose the areas you want to paint. Be sure to press the tape firmly to avoid bleeding, then roughen the exposed areas with fine sandpaper to ensure paint adhesion.

If you prefer, you can use strips of wall covering, as shown in the doorway *above*, to create an Art Deco entryway. Paint moldings first and let the overlaid wall covering provide the hard edge. Cut strips using a craft knife

against a metal ruler, and miter corners where strips meet so the design angles neatly around them.

Tape is all it took to turn a barren kitchen divider wall into a work of graphic art, *opposite*. The neat grid pattern, reinforced by the tile table, lends a sense of precision and order to the dining area, separating it visually as well as physically from the organized clutter of the kitchen work area. Measure carefully and rule squares using a level. Peel and press on the tape, doing small sections at a time to keep lines straight. You'll find many options in tape: assorted widths and colors as well as materials ranging from cloth and paper to metallics and plastics.

NEW LOOKS FROM A CAN OR BY THE ROLL

FOOL THE EYE

Fooling the eye into seeing what's not there has a long history in painting and decorating. The French coined a term for it: *trompe l'oeil,* deceiving the eye. You can devise your own eye-fooler with a custom enlargement of a favorite slide or with a strategically placed wallpaper mural or poster. The visual surprise of *trompe l'oeil* can add a playful touch or make a cramped space appear more open. If you're short on windows but long for a room with a view, you can create one like the picturesque outlook shown here.

Don't overlook potential illusions in your own photo album. Your favorite snapshot or color slide could become the *pièce de résistance* in any room. Line life-size images of your family down a hallway for a light touch, or grace a low ceiling with a view through tall trees.

A good custom lab can turn any photo or slide into a show-stopping wall mural. Would you like a lily pond wall-to-wall over the living room sofa? Choose a photo or slide and talk things over with the experts (who can also help with strategies for photography).

Merely mounting a super-size shot on the wall, however, doesn't always achieve maximum effect. For example, the view through the French doors at *right* is not the only great pretender. The architecture is unreal as well. Cut out and mounted 6 inches from the wall, this 8-foot-high impostor casts realistic shadows. Pots of real flowers help complete the illusion.

Photography tips
• Because the finished product can be no better than the original photograph, concentrate on shooting color *slides*. They make the best blowups.
• Fill the lens frame with the image. You'll get better composition and reproduction.
• Stick to standard paper sizes when you order your blowup. The process isn't cheap, and every extra inch costs more.
• When you're shooting an indoor/outdoor scene such as the French doors, close your lens down one more stop than your light meter reads. This will help balance indoor and outdoor light for realism. Late daytime is the best time to shoot such a scene.

• To increase the illusion of depth behind an opening such as the French door frame, use a wide-angle lens.
• For the best shots of architectural details (windows, doors, archways), hold the camera at the midway point of the object's height. Avoid "keystoning," or tilting the camera upward. The 8-foot-tall French doors were shot with the camera held at the 4-foot level.

More eye-fooling ideas
You may want to explore avenues other than blowups of prints and slides to create *trompe l'oeil* effects.
• Cut out pictures of canned goods and other foodstuffs, the bigger the better, and paste them on your cabinet fronts. Add a strip of tape to give them a shelf.
• Create a visual gag such as a hand turning on a light switch or holding up a shelf.
• Decorate a youngster's wall with a life-size cartoon character, or incorporate an object in the child's room (such as the bed) into a fantasy scene on the wall.
• Ask an outdoor advertising company for billboard photos that appeal to you.
• Browse through your library's photo collection.
• Check with movie theaters for large broadsides of film stars.
• Look for wallpaper covered with realistic, three-dimensional renderings of bookshelves filled with books, or of cupboards full of dishes. Or choose from a variety of wallpaper murals—gardens, landscapes, city skylines, and outdoor scenes—to open up a confining wall or to create a special effect.

TRY STENCILING

To create a beautifully stenciled wall or ceiling, you need paint, paper, and patience. You certainly *don't* need to be a formally trained artist. Some of the most charming stencil works from our Early American past were painted by itinerant handymen who just as readily would have mended a fence for their bed and board. Nevertheless, their designs were refreshing in their colorful naïveté, and many are available again today.

A number of museums and living-history villages have copied stencil patterns from their own historic walls and made the patterns available in kits for home craftsmen.

Contemporary stencil kits also are showing up on the shelves of paint and craft stores. Designs and colors are updated, but the process is the same, except that clear acrylic is replacing the traditional oiled stencil paper.

Of course, you can always design and cut your own stencil patterns. For example, try transferring the design from your bedspread or living room rug to your walls. You'll probably have to enlarge the original design to make it strong enough for the wall's expanse. Here's how:

First, trace the original on onionskin paper. Then, with carbon paper, transfer the pattern to ¼-inch graph paper; each square's side will equal 1 full inch when you scale up. Take a second sheet of graph paper and carefully duplicate the original drawing, but make it four times larger. (In linear measure, you'll draw four times as big, but in area, each square of the original will blow up to 16 squares.)

Transfer the full-size design to commercial stencil paper (available at paint or art supply stores) and cut it out with a utility knife. Leave sturdy "bridges," which are ⅛-inch-wide strips between the cutout shapes.

If you plan to lay down more than one color, make a separate stencil for each, with a "keyhole" to align successive stencils properly. These are called registration stencils. You might also work with modular stencils, which have only one stencil for each design.

Painting techniques

Acrylic paints dry quickly and provide a waterproof finish, characteristics that make them the most popular medium for stenciling. But you can experiment with other media, such as felt-tip pens or textile paints.

If you use paint, the right brush is essential for success. Stencil brushes that are round, with full, short bristles allow you to stipple the paint through the stencil cutouts. Hold the brush perpendicular to the surface. Never drag or stroke the brush, or the image will blur. Be sure the stencil is anchored firmly to the wall so paint doesn't run beneath it. Carefully lift the stencil and let the area dry before moving to the next section.

The photos at *right* show two of the steps leading to the stenciled border in the dining room *opposite*.

Akin to graphics and photographics, stenciling is an ancient decorating art that is undergoing a renaissance of interest in today's crafts-oriented homes. Here's how to give your walls a new look with this versatile, low-cost medium.

CHOOSING INTERIOR PAINT

Now that you've seen some of the decorating options that paint provides, let's look at the best ways to get these options out of the can and onto your walls and ceilings. Applying the paint correctly is only one part of the job. What you do before you paint is equally important. Choosing the appropriate paint for the effect you want, selecting the right tools for the job, and adequately preparing the surface to be painted will make the difference between a slapdash job and a professional-looking one.

Before you set out for a paint store, ask yourself these two important questions: (1) where will you be painting? (2) what color effect are you after?

Where you'll be painting largely determines the kind of paint you should buy. For almost all interior projects, your choices are either water- or solvent-thinned paints. Not that either is likely to need thinning. What matters is whether the paint cleans up with water or with a solvent such as mineral spirits.

- *Water-thinned* paints (you probably know them as latex paints) wipe off floors and wash out of tools with soap and water. They're fast-drying, nearly odorless, and pleasant to use. Their one drawback is that they are less durable than solvent-based paints.
- *Solvent-thinned* paints (sometimes called oil-base or alkyd paints) require cleaning with paint thinner. As a result, they're a bit more trouble to use, but you may prefer solvent-thinned paint where you need a longer-wearing surface.

Finishes
Both latex and alkyd paints come in three types of finishes: flat or low-gloss (also called satin, eggshell, or low-luster); semigloss; and high-gloss. Besides the difference in appearance, the finish determines how well the paint will wear. Hence, it dictates where you should use it.
- *Flat* paints generally work well on interior walls and ceilings. As a rule, they offer easier, better coverage than other finishes and cost less. The one catch: the duller the surface of the paint, the less resistance it offers to wear and washing.
- *Semigloss and high-gloss* paints protect doors, windows,

and other woodwork, as well as walls subject to especially hard wear, such as those in kitchens and baths.

Concerning color
Obtaining the exact color you want poses few problems because today's paints mix easily. However, color has a quirky side. It reacts to its environment, changing under different lighting conditions and in different surroundings. Thus, the turquoise chip you select under the store's fluorescent lights might become a warmer blue in the glow of your lamps at home. To be safe, buy a small quantity of the color you want and try it at home.

How much paint?
Paint manufacturers' labels will help you figure how much paint most jobs will take. The label usually states the one-coat coverage you can expect from one gallon of primer or paint. With that information, here are the measurements and calculations you will need to make:
- Measure the perimeter of the room (all walls) and multiply the result by the ceiling height to get the number of square feet. (Round off wall measurements to the next full foot.)
- Do not deduct for windows or other openings unless they add up to more than 100 square feet.
- Divide the result you get in the preceding step into the number of square feet a gallon of paint promises to cover (check the label). Rounding off to the next gallon gives you the number of gallons you'll need for your room. Double that number if you plan two coats.

Unless the label cautions against shaking the paint, ask your paint dealer to put each

can on a shaker. You'll have less stirring when you begin work. To assure color consistency, buy all the paint for your project at the same time.

Specialty paints
Specific jobs and some special effects require paints made just for that purpose.
- *One-coat* latex or alkyd paints can be used on surfaces that are already sealed and have little patchwork to be blended in. Additional pigment increases their hiding power, but also adds to the price.
- *Texture* paints let you cover up imperfections in wall surfaces and create the effect of stucco, among others. Some come premixed; with others you stir in a silica sand additive. Application is moderately difficult, and it takes time to work out the desired pattern.
- *Acoustic* paints let you cover acoustic tile surfaces without impairing their sound-absorbing qualities. They come in a limited number of colors and are sprayed on or applied with a special roller.
- *Dripless* paints make ceiling painting easier and reduce clean-up time, but you'll pay extra for this convenience.

About primers
A primer seals surfaces and provides "tooth" to hold new paint. Apply a primer if: (1) you are painting a raw surface (one that has never been painted or sealed before); (2) you are making a significant change in color, such as from dark to light or light to dark; or (3) you are covering a glossy surface with a latex paint or latex with alkyd.

The primer you need depends on the kind of paint you use. Read the label or consult your paint dealer.

YOUR PAINT OPTIONS

	USES	DURABILITY	THINNER/PRIMER
LATEX	Comes in flat, semigloss, and high-gloss finishes. Choose flat for most walls and ceilings; semigloss or high-gloss for woodwork, furniture, and kitchen and bathroom walls. Don't use on unprimed wood, metal, or wallpaper.	Tolerates moderate abuse but flat-finish latex paints do not stand up to repeated scrubbings as well as semigloss and high-gloss. The alkyds wear better.	Water-thinned. Cleans up with ease. A damp rag removes spills; soap and water clean rollers, brushes, and your hands. On raw surfaces, use latex or alkyd primer first.
ALKYD AND OIL	These terms are used almost interchangeably, although true natural-resin oil paint has all but disappeared. Alkyds provide a tough surface and cover well. Good for walls (except unprimed drywall), ceilings, woodwork, kitchen and bath walls.	Alkyds dry a bit more slowly than latex; oil paints dry very slowly (and give off a characteristic odor in the process). Alkyds are tougher than latex; oils are less durable. Use semigloss or high-gloss in high-wear areas.	Solvents (mineral spirits or odorless thinners) are required for cleanup if you use alkyds. Oil-base paints call for turpentine or other mineral spirits. Use alkyd primer for alkyd paint. Follow the label if you use oils.
URETHANE, POLYURETHANE, AND EPOXY	Urethane and polyurethane put a super-tough finish on almost any porous surface or on any finish. Epoxy will put a new face on otherwise unpaintable surfaces such as glass, tile, and porcelain. Epoxy won't adhere to an already-painted finish.	Plastic-base urethanes and polyurethanes are color-carrying cousins of the clear polyurethane varnishes that make floors impervious to dirt, grease, abrasion, even alcohol. Epoxy is the strongest and most expensive paint.	Urethane, polyurethane, and epoxy paints are thinned with solvents. Check the manufacturer's recommendations for the right solvent and primer.
SPECIALTY PAINTS	**One-coat.** Latex or alkyd paints with extra pigment for extra covering ability. More expensive than ordinary paint.	One-coat paints wear as well as ordinary paints. Use only on pre-sealed surfaces with minimal patchwork and color difference.	Cleans up with water or solvent like other latex and alkyd paints.
	Texture. Gives walls, ceiling the look of stucco.	Comes premixed, or with sandlike powder that stirs in. Patience, practice required.	No thinning: The intent is to look thick and stuccolike. Consult label for primers.
	Acoustic. Doesn't impair acoustical qualities of tile.	Requires spraying or special roller. Limited colors.	Washes up with soap and water; doesn't need priming.
	Dripless. A boon for painting ceilings.	Costs extra but saves drips, especially down your arms.	Water- or solvent-base. Consult label for priming.
	Metal. For primed or bare metals.	Self-primers that adhere well to bare metal surfaces.	Both water- and solvent-base. The kind of metal dictates the primer.

41

THE RIGHT WAY TO PAINT A ROOM

You've probably heard this before, but it's worth repeating: A finished paint job is only as good as the preparation work. Painted surfaces, especially high-gloss surfaces, exaggerate blemishes in walls or woodwork, so take the time to patch holes, scrape away peeling paint, sand everything smooth, and put on a coat of primer if needed. After you apply the finish coat, you'll be glad you invested the additional effort.

You will be able to paint over wall coverings if they adhere smoothly to the walls and if seams are tight. However, slick wall coverings such as vinyls and metallics require a primer. Use latex over most wall coverings. Before starting, paint a test area to be sure colors and blemishes will not bleed through. Also do the following things before you paint:
- Remove light switch plates.
- Remove light fixtures or cover them.
- Wipe the walls with a dry mop.
- Wash kitchen and bath walls to remove grease and dirt. Allow them to dry completely before you paint.

Tooling up for the task

If you ask a professional, you'll learn that the right tools make the job easier. What makes a brush or roller the right one? Quality is an important factor. Buy the best you can afford, especially if you hope to use the tool again.

Brushes come in many sizes and shapes, but their bristles are either natural or synthetic. Natural animal hair brushes once were vastly superior to man-made bristles, but that is no longer true.

To judge the quality of either type, check the tips of the bristles. They should look fuzzy, because those little "flags" help hold the paint. Test to see that the bristles aren't molting badly. A loose bristle or two is natural; any more will spoil your efforts. Test the brush for heft. Will you be comfortable holding it for several hours? Be sure the ferrule, the band that binds the bristles, is wrapped tightly and is solidly attached to the handle.

Bristle brushes aren't your only option. Disposable foam brushes and painting pads reduce clean-up time. Rollers cover large, flat surfaces faster than brushes. Although many people prefer a brush for painting small, tight areas such as trim, you can get rollers sized and shaped to handle even those jobs. The manufacturer usually labels the handle of brushes and rollers to indicate the best matching of finishes and tools. If there is no label, remember these rules:
- For oil-base paint, use a natural-bristle or a good-quality synthetic (preferably nylon) brush, or a roller that has a cardboard sleeve and a cover made of Dynel, acetate, polyurethane foam, or lamb's wool.
- For water-thinned paints, use synthetic bristles only, or a roller with a plastic sleeve. The roller can be covered with any of the materials listed above except lamb's wool.

One further word about rollers. Covers have naps of $\frac{1}{16}$ to $\frac{1}{2}$ inch. The long ones are meant for rough surfaces; the short naps lay down a smooth coat.

PAINTING STEPS

1 Prepare woodwork by tightening loose trim, using finishing nails and a nail set. Fill holes and blemishes with putty. Remove hardware, sand smooth, and sponge clean.

2 Tools needed for roller painting include a slant-bottom roller pan, a roller (with an extra cover for quick color changes), a brush for cutting in ceiling lines and painting trim, and a few plastic drop cloths to minimize cleanup (top drop cloths with newspapers so spills don't puddle).

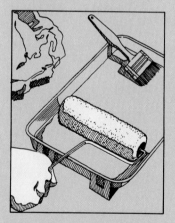

3 Pour in enough paint to fill about half of the slant-bottom portion of the pan. To load the roller, roll it into the lower end of the pan, then smooth out the paint load on the slanted surface. The goal is to carry as much paint as you can to the wall without dripping.

4 To paint the upper reaches of walls without a ladder, add a handle extension to the roller. (Extensions are available at paint stores. Some extensions screw in; others come with a collar.) Use the brush to cut in the ceiling line.

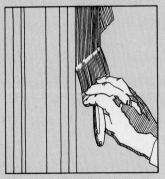

5 Use the brush for edging around woodwork at doors and windows. If you're applying latex or alkyd flat paints, you can do the brushwork around the entire room in advance. With these paints, lapmarks don't show.

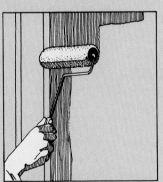

6 Return to the roller and blend in the brushwork by running the roller as close to the woodwork as possible. Some rollers have guards to prevent smearing the trim. Run the roller fairly dry before taking this step.

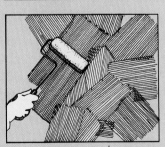

7 Apply paint to the main wall area by rolling out a big "M" and filling in the voids. Roll in all directions for best coverage, but not so fast that you spin off a spray of paint droplets.

8 Small rollers make short work of once-tedious jobs such as most trim work. Intricate woodwork still requires a brush, but you can use a roller on door trim, for instance. Keep the roller fairly dry so paint doesn't build up on cross members and stiles.

9 Use a regular roller to paint the door panels and large flat cross members. If you haven't removed the hardware, you'll need a brush to work around the hardware and the knob.

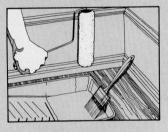

10 You'll bless the roller's speed again when you come to the baseboards. After edging the top of the molding and the base shoe with the brush, zip right down the middle of the molding with the roller.

11 To cut the tedium of painting window trim, drive a nail lightly into the bottom of each sash so you can easily raise and lower it to get at the angles. Use a razor-blade scraper to clean up splatters later.

12 Wash roller and brush in water (for latex) or in a solvent such as turpentine (for alkyds). Squeeze both thoroughly and shape the brush. Let both dry before packing them in paper towels and plastic bags.

CHOOSING WALL COVERINGS

Wall coverings are back in style, in part because new materials and new manufacturing techniques put things squarely in the hands of do-it-yourselfers. You probably recall the old gags about hanging wallpaper, all to the effect that you end up hanging yourself rather than the paper. The job is no longer the exclusive province of seasoned professionals. A handy amateur can now choose from a range of wall covering options. The following pages show you what's available, and the advantages and disadvantages of each type.

Begin by mastering the vocabulary of wall coverings. Understanding the language helps when you're looking through sample books.

• *Prepasted wall coverings.* A big boon to do-it-yourselfers, prepasted goods eliminate most of the mess that used to accompany hanging wall coverings. The manufacturer coats the back with dry glue; you dip each roll in water and apply it to the wall.

• *Pretrimmed wall coverings.* At one time all wall coverings came with white borders called *selvages.* These protected the pattern during shipping and handling, but it took a steady hand to trim them off during installation. Now, with the exception of a few costly hand prints, nearly all wall coverings come from the manufacturer pretrimmed.

• *Strippable wall coverings.* Strippable coverings have adhesives and strong facing materials that allow them to be peeled off the wall without steaming, wetting, or scraping. However, you cannot rehang the covering once you have stripped it.

• *Wall covering squares.* An old idea whose time has come again (once all wallpapers were only small squares), these 12x12-inch modules simplify hanging. They are prepasted, so you dip them in a dishpan and slip them onto the wall. They are especially handy for small areas such as kitchens, closets, and baths. Each square contains a complete design motif, eliminating the chance of mismatching patterns.

• *Washable/scrubbable wall coverings.* There is a substantial difference between washable and scrubbable. If a wall covering is stamped ''washable,'' you can wipe soil from the surface with a damp cloth and perhaps a little mild soap. If a covering is ''scrubbable,'' you can go after dirt, grease, and smoke stains with vigor, time after time, without damaging the surface.

What's your type?

You've probably noticed that the word wallpaper rarely appears in this chapter. That's because paper is only one of the coverings you can choose to add pattern, color, and texture to a room. Although they all come in rolls, often prepasted and pretrimmed, wall coverings may be any of the following:

• *Fabrics.* Choose from silks, linens, and brocades for formal rooms. Select burlap, corduroy, and mini-calico prints for informal schemes. Textures in neutral tones add wall interest to contemporary settings. Among the newest of the textured coverings are ''strings,'' real strings laid over plain or patterned backgrounds for a soft, three-dimensional effect.

• *Vinyls.* Laminated to cloth or paper backings (see the chart on page 45), vinyl wall coverings can be slick and shiny, or they can resemble many other materials: damask, linen, wood. In whatever guise, vinyls are easy to care for.

• *Metallics.* Foils and Mylars put any room in a reflective mood. Just be sure the wall is in nearly perfect shape, because metallics highlight even small irregularities.

• *Flocks.* Flocked wall coverings are velvet to the touch, damask or cut velvet to the eye. The technique of flocking paper with finely cut fibers is being revived as a textural option for contemporary settings.

• *Natural cork/real woods.* Sliced wafer-thin and attached to flexible backings, they add natural color and earthy texture and are a good choice for hiding wall imperfections. Wood coverings can work on walls with unusual contours that would be difficult to panel.

• *Grass cloth.* Made of synthetic or natural grass fibers laminated to paper, grass cloth has a woven look similar to burlap, only coarser. It is more expensive than most coverings, but adds an elegant touch. Use with lining papers for best results.

• *Liners.* Lining papers, wall coverings' counterpart to paint primer, are worth the extra time for hanging if you install an expensive or delicate covering, or if your walls are so rough that defects are likely to show through the new covering. A special liner for covering cinder blocks is available, as well as a thick foam liner that provides some insulation.

YOUR WALL COVERING OPTIONS

	USES	DURABILITY	COST
WALLPAPERS	**Machine-printed.** Produced on high-speed presses. Considerable quality at reasonable cost. At home anywhere in the house.	Paper is delicate; a vinyl coating lengthens its life. Takes a damp cloth but not serious scrubbing.	Inexpensive to moderate; $10 or more per roll.
	Hand-printed. Printed by hand on paper, linen, vinyl, foil, silk, with giant silk screens. Custom coloring available. Install where wear is minimal.	Fragile but wipable; follow manufacturer's advice.	Expensive; about $75 for a single roll.
	Lining. Base for foils, Mylar, grass cloth, other specialty coverings. A must if walls are rough or worn.	Prolongs looks, life of covering.	Inexpensive. About $10 per roll.
VINYLS	**Vinyl-coated.** Thin layer of vinyl on machine-printed papers protects the design and makes hanging easier. Avoid damp areas.	Durable in moderate-use areas but not the best choice for baths or kitchens.	Wide range of prices.
	Paper-backed. Durable vinyl facing laminated to a paper backing. Printed or embossed to look like fabrics.	Tough enough to shrug off dirt, stains, and physical abuse; scrubbable.	From moderate up.
	Fabric-backed. Vinyl laminated to fabric to make an exceptionally heavy and hard-wearing wall cover.	The toughest. Perfect for humid baths and grease-prone kitchens; takes repeated scrubbings.	From moderate up.
SPECIALTY WALL COVERINGS	**Fabrics.** From silks to coarse homespuns, can cover any wall and provide a small amount of noise insulation.	Avoid installing where moisture or excessive soiling is likely.	Expensive. As high as $100 a roll.
	Flocks. Add the look of cut velvet to traditional rooms, or textural interest in contemporary designs.	Flocking wears off in rooms where people are likely to brush against the wall.	More costly than plain coverings.
	Grass Cloth. An elegant choice, woven of real grasses or vinyl-embossed look-alikes.	Soils easily.	Expensive; $40 or more.
	Metallics. Thin sheets of flexible metal (foil or Mylar) that serve as backgrounds for prints. Mirror surfaces expand space.	Good for baths, kitchens, and laundry areas because of washability. May show dents. Wipe clean.	Moderate to high-priced.

PUTTING UP WALL COVERINGS

Many professionals advise stripping off all old wallpaper before putting up new. You don't have to *if* the old wallpaper is tight. If it's not, try cutting out the loose sections and piecing in patches to make the surface flush.

Nobody wants the messy job of stripping an entire wall or room, but if there's no alternative, take heart. You can rent a wallpaper steamer and save hours of soaking and scraping. Hold the steam plate against each section, and remove it with a scraper. Once you've removed all the old paper, wash the walls and let them dry thoroughly before you begin anew.

Painted walls present few problems. If the paint has a glossy finish, use an abrasive or coat the wall with sizing to dull the gloss so the adhesive will stick securely.

How much wall covering?

You can purchase wall coverings by the *bolt*, which may contain a single, double, or triple roll. Each roll contains 30 square feet of coverage.

To estimate the number of rolls you need, measure the distance around the room, including nooks, crannies, and door openings. Then measure the height of the ceiling. Multiply the ceiling height by the distance around the room (round off to the nearest foot) and divide by 30. From this figure, subtract one-half roll for each normal-size window and door. The result (rounded to the next whole number) is the number of rolls you need.

If you plan to cover the ceiling or use borders, take a sketch of your floor plan (with measurements) to your dealer, who can translate the figures into the proper number of rolls.

Tools and adhesives

The type of wall covering you buy will determine both the adhesive and the tools you need to hang it. With prepasted covering, you won't need any adhesive, just a water box into which you dip the covering. Strippable products require a *wheat* or *strippable adhesive*. Standard wallpapers call for *wheat* or *stainless adhesives*. Foils, vinyls, flocks, hand prints, and others necessitate *vinyl adhesive*, available ready-mixed in containers. Choose one that resists mildew.

For all wall covering jobs, you'll need a few special tools: a level, a seam roller, a smoothing brush, a lot of single-edge razor blades, a plumb bob and chalk line, long sharp scissors, a yardstick, a wide metal scraper, an 8-foot straightedge or piece of aluminum angle (for guiding the razor when you trim excess material), and a couple of sponges.

To hang unpasted wall coverings, you also need a paste brush and a pan (a plastic dishpan works well), and a long pasting table. A couple of chairs with a board or door resting on them will work, or rent a table from your wall covering dealer.

Tips from the pros

Here's how to make your job go fast and look professional.
• Plan to finish in an inconspicuous corner because the pattern usually does not match on the final strip.
• Uncurl a couple of rolls by drawing them across a table edge, then weight the rolls so they lie flat on the floor until you need them.
• Work clean. Wash up often, and never let adhesive dry on the face of the wall covering.

HANGING PAPER

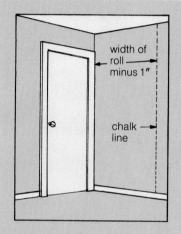

width of roll minus 1"

chalk line

1 You must get the first strip absolutely straight because it determines alignment all around the room. Start at a door or in a corner; snap a plumb chalk line on the wall at a distance equal to the width of the wall covering, minus 1 inch. Check plumb with a level.

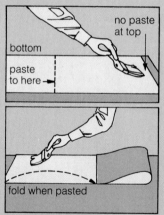

bottom

paste to here

no paste at top

fold when pasted

2 Cut the first strip of wall covering several inches longer than the height of the wall. Working on the pasting table, apply adhesive to *half* of the strip, leaving about 1 inch unpasted at the top so you can hold it. Fold over, then paste the other half and fold it over, too.

3 Unfold the top half of the pasted strip, align the right edge with the plumb line, and smooth the top to the wall with your hands. Let the unpasted top inch or so overlap onto the ceiling. If the other edge looks crooked in the corner or against the door, the room itself is probably out of plumb.

4 Now unfold the lower half and smooth it on the wall. Use a level or a plumb line to make sure it is straight. If it is not, try the operation again. If the covering is straight, use your smoothing brush vigorously. Work from the center out.

5 When this first strip adheres tightly to the wall with no air bubbles under it, use the end of the brush to press the covering securely into the corners. Trim with a razor blade or utility knife.

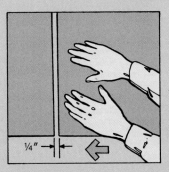

6 Matching the pattern to the first strip, cut several more strips at one time, numbering them as you cut. As you hang the strips, butt by aligning one strip about ¼ inch from the adjoining one, then slide the strip until the edges meet tightly.

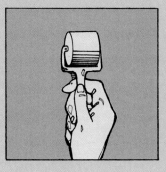

7 About 15 minutes after hanging each strip, roll the seams to make sure they are flat. *Do not* roll flocks, Mylars, foils, and grass cloths; rolling them will crush the finish. Instead, tap the seams with your fingers or a brush.

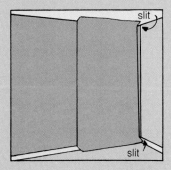

8 Never wrap wall covering around a corner. Instead, measure from the edge of the last strip to the corner and cut a piece ½ inch wider. Paste, align with previous strip, and hang, bending only the ½-inch margin around the corner. Trim into the margin, top and bottom, if needed.

9 To get out of the corner, snap a plumb line on the second wall, allowing for overlap onto the ½-inch margin and ½-inch back around the corner. When you hang the new strip, tap the edge securely into the corner, overlapping the margin.

10 In the corner, double-cut through both thicknesses. Peel off the strip on one side, then lift the edge and peel away the inner layer. Smooth both edges and roll the seam. This technique compensates for corners that are out of plumb, as most are.

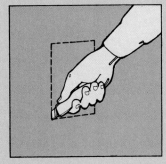

11 Remove cover plates, but paper right over receptacles and switches, then trim. Never let foils come in contact with outlets. With any material, always shut off the power before you trim the excess.

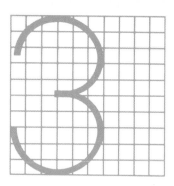

EASY-CARE SURFACES

The allure of easy-care materials is compelling: If you dress a wall in wood, glass, metal, brick, or tile, you can forget about painting, heavy cleaning, and most other routine maintenance chores. High durability makes each of these surfaces a lifetime investment, one that will dramatically enhance the appearance of your home while you live there and add to its value if you decide to sell. This chapter explores all the easy-care options and shows how most are also easy to install.

MANUFACTURED PANELING

Nothing quite matches the mellow warmth of a paneled room. If long life, low maintenance, and easy installation are all on your list of musts, few wall materials score higher than manufactured paneling.

Manufactured paneling falls into two general categories: plywood and processed wood fibers. Plywood panels are often veneered with genuine hardwood or softwood that is prefinished to enhance grain, texture, and color. Less expensive plywood paneling has a vinyl or paper overlay that simulates wood grains.

Processed wood fiber panels are made up as hardboard, particleboard, or waferboard. Hardboard and particleboard consist of compressed sawdust or wood chips bonded with glue and faced with vinyl or paper overlays. Waferboard is manufactured from thin slices of genuine wood and has no overlay.

All manufactured paneling comes in standard 4x8-foot sheets. If your ceiling is higher than 8 feet, you can special-order 9- or 10-foot lengths, or piece in above the 8-foot line and cover the gap with molding, as was done in the room shown *opposite*. The grooves in manufactured paneling appear to be spaced randomly, but you'll always find one spaced at intervals of 16 and 24 inches so you can inconspicuously nail into studs or furring strips.

However, you don't need a lot of nails. Paneling adhesives that you squeeze from a caulking gun do most of the support work. Those large sheets go up fast with a minimum of cutting, piecing, and fitting, which is one reason why manufactured paneling appears to have been designed with do-it-yourselfers in mind.

(Pages 56-59 take you step by step through the process of putting up paneling and other sheet goods.)

A lot to choose from
Whatever your style, from country casual to city slick, paneling is probably available to suit your taste. Manufactured panelings offer finishes, whether they're light or dark, glossy or textured, that are difficult to distinguish from wood. However, you aren't limited to the look of wood. Alternate facings come in solid colors or patterns that simulate fabric, tile, and marble.

Prices vary widely from inexpensive printed hardboards to costly imported veneers. (For more about choosing and buying paneling, see pages 54 and 55.)

Caring for paneling
Factory finishes assure easily maintained walls that last for years with only minimal attention. Wiping with a damp cloth removes most household grime. Tougher dirt calls for a mild detergent solution. Prefinished surfaces have fair resistance to scratching, and minor blemishes can be covered with color-matched crayons available from manufacturers. Deep gouges are a problem, however, because if you try to spot-sand and refinish a section, it won't blend in. With major damage the best aproach is to remove and replace an entire panel, as explained on pages 148 and 149.

BOARDS
AND STRIPS

Manufactured sheet goods are the easiest and most popular way to panel a room, but they aren't the only way. If you'd like the warmth, beauty, and aesthetic satisfaction of the real thing, consider boards or strips of solid wood. Thicker than plywood or pressed fiber panels, they are natural insulators. Boards and strips offer a broader choice of finishes, too, from super-shiny to matte to the natural look of unfinished wood. When it comes to design effects, solid wood is one of the most versatile materials you'll find.

The difference between boards and strips is size. Both are cut less than 2 inches thick, but boards are more than 3 inches wide, while strips are less than 3 inches wide. (Planks, a third lumber category, are 2 or more inches thick and are rarely used in paneling applications.)

These are nominal dimensions, not actual. Actual sizes are typically about ¼ inch less in thickness, and ½ or ¾ inch less in width. Hence, a 1x4 board actually measures ¾x3½ inches; a 1x12 is ¾x11¼ inches.

Both boards and strips come with either square or interlocking edges in random or specified lengths up to 20 feet. Cedar, fir, pine, cypress, mahogany, rosewood—your choice of species ranges almost as widely as wood itself, but you can expect to pay dearly for more exotic woods. You needn't limit yourself to brand-new wood. Oak strips on the entry and kitchen walls, *opposite*, originally covered the home's floors. Carefully removed, stripped, and reused, they now gleam with new life. (More about recycling wood on pages 52 and 53.)

Pattern possibilities
Part of solid wood's magic is its adaptability. In the entry and kitchen at *left*, for instance, bold grain and warm coloring mellow a starkly contemporary decor, yet the same wood, also applied horizontally, would be equally at home in a country setting.

Vertical, diagonal, even herringbone patterns are worth considering. Let your room's architectural details and angles dictate the layout. Horizontal lines appear to widen a room and lower the ceiling. Vertical boards or strips have the opposite effect, drawing the eye upward.

Horizontals and verticals are easier to install, but the rewards of a finely executed craft await anyone who can master a diagonal or herringbone design. The photo at *right* illustrates one way to use diagonals. Instead of butting edges tightly together, the owners first painted the original wall in a dark color, then spaced 1x4s ½ inch apart. The dark gaps between boards add dimension and compensate for minor warping and irregularities along the edges of the boards. (More about putting up diagonal, herringbone, and other patterns on pages 60 and 61.)

Installing boards and strips
Before you get out a hammer, allow wood to adjust to the environment of the room. This process, which takes at least 48 hours, minimizes expansion or shrinkage later. Lay out the boards and strips in the order in which you'll put them up. Randomly mix grains, lengths, and colors for the effects you want. Some lumber comes with two surfaces, smooth and rough-sawn; decide which you want to face out.

Solid wood is heavier than sheet goods, so don't expect to be able to install it with glue alone. You'll also need nails, which means locating wall studs or putting up furring (explained on pages 56 and 57).

Finishing solid wood
Most sheet goods come prefinished, but lumber does not,

which gives you a wide range of options. Clear penetrating sealers or semi-transparent stains accent and protect woods. You may want to leave some species, such as redwood or cedar, unfinished so you can enjoy the wood's natural highlights. Cedar and redwood are good choices for baths and other damp areas because they are not adversely affected by moisture.

(Other lumbers can be left natural, too, but need to be

sealed against warping with paste wax.) For a country look, try paint. It can be brushed on and left to dry, or wiped off with a cloth, leaving streaks of color that accentuate the grain.

Maintenance
Solid wood requires an initial investment in money and installation labor, but needs minimal care once it's up. Light dusting usually will suffice, supplemented with occasional cleaning in high-use areas. Natural resin oil surfaces should be oiled periodically.

BARN BOARDS AND SHAKES

Not many of us can resist the charm of materials touched by nature's hand. And few of nature's materials evoke a warmer feeling than cedar shakes or weathered old barn boards. Shakes combine rustic good looks with rugged durability. Weather-silvered barn boards remind us of country life or the western prairies. Beautiful, natural, and needing almost no upkeep, both of these exterior materials bring unusual looks to interior spaces.

Unlike other woods, old barn boards don't grow on trees. If you can find a farmer with a dilapidated barn or other outbuilding that he'll let you tear down, count yourself fortunate. Scarcity and popularity have driven up the price of used lumber, a fact of economic life most farmers already know.

You may have to pay a premium to an architectural salvage firm, or seek out urban sources such as city sheds or garages.

Most of us think of old barn siding as the perfect backdrop for a collection of antiques. But in the home *above,* a bold stroke brings together old barn wood and contemporary materials in an up-to-the-minute kitchen. The contrast of crisp white counters, wall, and ceiling with the rough and rustic boards makes this room an eclectic success. Each horizontal piece of wood has been cut from a lone plank and then matched to harmonize colors and grain. A coating of clear plastic protects the wood.

Board magic
Sprucing up moss- or dirt-covered lumber may seem an awesome task, but a little elbow grease will do the job. Scrub the wood with a stiff brush and detergent suds. Rinse it well with a garden hose, then wash with household disinfectant. Allow boards to dry in the sun or in a warm place. Don't worry about streaks of paint that may linger in crevices; they lend an authentic touch. To remove large or unsightly patches, use a wire brush.

If your wood came from the *interior* rather than exterior of the barn, it is probably smoother. To finish, brush on and rub in linseed oil. *Exterior* planks will darken if finished, so try leaving them unfinished to retain their silver-gray sheen.

Installing planks
Because of the weight of these boards (considerably heavier than plywood) don't secure them with paneling adhesive. Instead, nail the boards to furring strips attached to the wall (see pages 56 and 57). If you're applying boards to basement walls, place a vapor barrier behind them. A side benefit is that those thick boards help keep rooms warm in winter, cool in summer, and quiet year-round.

Shake up your space
The rustic retreat shown at *right* has a woodsy atmosphere you can almost smell. The etched shadows and rich red tone of the shake wall set the mood—contemporary, casual, and cozy. A rope rail and tree-trunk coat rack create a treehouse atmosphere.

More often applied to exteriors, cedar shakes have natural resistance to weathering and to decay. When used indoors, their rustic and rugged qualities help set an easy-going mood.

Apply shakes to furring strips, beginning the first course at the floor line. Nail at upper corners. A double course, one layer on top of the next, will cast a deeper shadow. You can apply shakes in a uniform or random pattern. Either will create an interesting design. Stain, clear sealant, and unfinished treatments are possible finishes.

CHOOSING AND BUYING PANELING

When you set out to shop for paneling, you can easily get lost in the forest of wood products available as wall coverings. You'll find dozens of different types, textures, and wood tones. Prices vary widely, from economical hardboards to costly veneers. And there's the important matter of figuring exactly how much material you need. Clearly, the place to start shopping is at home. Here are the questions to ask yourself and the measurements you'll need to make a paneling purchase.

One of the first questions to ask yourself about any paneling job is what do you want the wood to do? If you're looking for nothing more than a quick, inexpensive coverup or change of appearance, by all means use an economical hardboard or particleboard material. On the other hand, if appearance and durability are paramount, you might want to invest in quality plywood or solid lumber. Here's an overview of the three main categories.

• *Plywood* divides into two main groups: panels veneered with genuine hardwood and panels covered with embossed, color-toned, or simulated woodgrain patterns. Face veneers on the first group usually derive from domestic sources. On the second group the veneers are usually imitations of more costly imported species. They don't look as natural as genuine veneers, of course, but new manufacturing techniques produce simulated panels that come close to the real thing. A sharp eye can detect, however, that woodgrain patterns repeat themselves from panel to panel.

• *Wood fiber* paneling falls into two general categories: Hardboard and particleboard make up one category, and waferboard is the other. The first two are usually faced with textured or printed overlays that, like simulated-veneer plywood panels, repeat every four feet. Waferboard is composed of large thin wafers of genuine wood and each sheet has its own unique grain pattern. You can stain or paint waferboard, leave it natural, or give it a clear finish.

• *Solid boards* or strips of flooring offer the ultimate in wood-grain flexibility, along with a surface that says "thunk" when you rap it with your knuckles. Solid wood is more difficult to put up, however, and the costs of some species rival or exceed the cost of top-of-the-line plywood panels.

Sizing up paneling needs

At today's prices you don't want to buy more paneling than you need. With veneers and solid stock you don't want to come up short, either, because you might not be able to match appearance exactly with paneling from a later shipment. Fortunately, computing an accurate materials list isn't difficult, but it takes a little time.

First, analyze what you need to do. Is this a complete overhaul or just a minor tune-up? Do you want to create an accent wall to put verve into a drab corner, or are you trying to conceal walls that are deteriorating?

Usually you can nail or glue paneling directly to a wall. But if you're building new walls, you'll have to cover studs with drywall first. Paneling is not an effective sound or fire retardant, and many building codes require drywall to be put up first.

Next, lay out the project on graph paper. With a scale drawing, you can count squares to compute the exact number of paneling sheets you'll need. Make elevation drawings of each wall, showing windows, doors, offsets,

electrical outlets, and pipes. Use 4x8-foot scaled cutouts made of graph paper to figure the number of panels each wall surface will require. Simply lay the cutouts down on your wall diagrams. This way, you'll see exactly where to cut panels for windows, electrical outlets, corners, and so on. Just be sure to double-check your measurements before you cut the panels.

If you're paneling with solid boards or strips, total the number of square feet you'll need, then add 10 percent for cutting waste.

Selecting trim

Use your scale drawing to calculate the number of lineal feet of molding you'll need at the ceiling, floor, corners, door frames, and window casings. Some sheet goods manufacturers offer prefinished moldings that harmonize with their paneling. With others—and with all solid lumber—you'll need to buy unfinished moldings and stain or varnish them to match.

Here are the most common types of molding and trim:

• *Base* molding (baseboard) is used at the bottom of walls to provide a smooth transition from wall to floor.

• *Casing* is the flat trim that frames door and window openings.

• *Outside/inside corner* molding is used to cover the ragged edges of paneling at corners.

• *Cove* molding is applied at the top of walls to provide a smooth transition from paneling to ceiling.

• *Stool* is the flat, horizontal member that forms the sill at the base of windows.

• *Mullion* is a narrow strip used between pairs of windows or closely spaced doors.

YOUR PANELING OPTIONS

MATERIAL	CHOICES	FEATURES	COST
PLYWOOD	Prefinished panelings are made with genuine hardwood and softwood face veneers, and with realistic color-toned, embossed, and simulated woodgrain finishes. A variety of wood species, groove patterns, and textures is available. Finish treatments may be high- or low-gloss acrylic coating or a more rustic, unfinished appearance.	Plywood panels come in standard 4x8-foot sheets (you must special-order 9- and 10-foot lengths) ranging from ¼ inch to $7/16$ inch in thickness. Most have three-ply construction and durable factory finishes. Easy for do-it-yourself installation; apply panels directly over drywall or use furring strips on uneven surfaces. Wipe clean with a damp cloth. Don't use in high-moisture areas.	Generally, panelings with a simulated woodgrain finish are less expensive than genuine wood-veneered panels. Decorative hardboard and softwood face veneers are the top of the line, but prices vary widely according to type of wood. Printed or plywood-overlaid panels are moderate in price, an excellent choice for almost any type of decorating project.
WOOD FIBER	Processed wood fiber wall panelings are available in three basic types: hardboard, particleboard, and waferboard. Particleboard and hardboard panels may have grain-printed paper overlays or printed faces. Waferboard panels offer a wood-textured surface that can be painted, stained, clear-varnished, or left natural.	Hardboard and particleboard are processed from wood residue into solid, smooth boards. Waferboard is made from large, thin wafers of hardwood. All are available in 4x8-foot sheets in thicknesses from ¼ inch to $5/16$ inch. Waferboard has no core voids, knots, or splits, and can be used in high-moisture areas; do *not* use hardboard and particleboard in humid zones.	Wood fiber panels are considerably lower in price than solid boards or prefinished plywood paneling. Hardboard, particleboard, and waferboard are economical choices for all types of projects. Their low-to-moderate price appeals to budget-minded shoppers.
SOLID BOARDS AND STRIPS	From old barn wood to clear redwood, the selection in solid board panels is as varied as the trees they come from. Softwood varieties are available in a dozen or more species, including cedar, redwood, fir, and pine; popular hardwood boards include oak and birch. Strips, typically used for flooring, are available in oak, maple, and fir.	Board sizes vary from ⅜ inch thick to ¾ inch. Edges are square, tongue-and-groove, or shiplapped. No. 2 and No. 3 common boards are used for paneling, but No. 1 commons are the highest grade. Installation requires better carpentry skills than for sheet paneling, but design possibilities are greater. Apply with finishing nails. Stain, paint, oil, varnish, or leave natural.	Prices of solid boards vary from moderate to quite expensive. Species, grade of wood, and regional availability are factors in pricing. Used lumber and boards sometimes can be purchased at bargain rates, but usable barn siding is soaring in price. To save, buy the lowest grade of board that will do the job, and the smallest quantity possible.

INSTALLING
PANELING

Just as you need a firm foundation before you can build a house, so you must have a solid backing before you put up paneling. If you install panels over a surface that is anything but sound and even, the panels eventually will warp, crack, or even pull off the wall. Here's how to check your walls and remedy any ills they might have.

Start by removing all trim and molding around the ceiling, floors, windows, and doors. If you plan to reuse molding, protect it by storing it outside the room in which you will work.

Scrutinize the surfaces you'll be dealing with. Shine a strong light on each wall and sight along it, looking for bulges, depressions, or waviness. Double-check by holding a long, straight 2x4 against the wall at various angles. If you see hollows under the 2x4, or if it rocks at some points, you'll have to even the walls with furring strips before you panel. Look for signs of decay or moisture. Correct these problems before going on.

If your walls pass inspection, wash them with a household cleanser and start paneling, as explained on pages 58-61.

If your walls aren't smooth, or if you'll be working with masonry surfaces, you need to add furring strips, which are lengths of 1x2s or 1x3s, to achieve a solid, even base.

(If you're paneling a basement or garage, consider building a 2x4 or 2x3 stud framework rather than putting up furring. Studs allow more space for insulation, electrical outlets, and pipes.)

Tools you'll need for furring include a tape measure, carpenter's level, plumb bob, stud finder, crosscut saw, drills and bits, nail set, pencil compass, keyhole saw, caulking gun, and rubber mallet. Besides the furring strips, get a small supply of wood shingles to use for shimming. *(continued)*

FURRING OUT WALLS

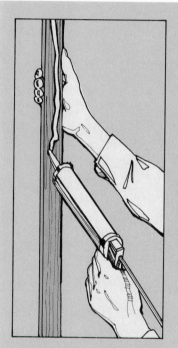

1 Mark locations for vertical furring strips on the wall. To do this, place a sheet of paneling in a corner of the room, plumb it, and draw a line on the wall along the panel's outside edge. Using the line as a guide, measure 16-inch increments along the rest of the wall on both sides of the original line. Lines at these points position the vertical strips. Now measure and cut each strip (one at a time) to fit from floor to ceiling. Apply a ¼-inch bead of panel adhesive down one side of the first strip as shown.

2 Place the furring strip on the first mark. *Center* the strip on the line, pressing it firmly into place to help spread the adhesive evenly. If you are furring over a masonry wall, first apply a coat of waterproof sealant before furring out. Even the best paneling is not moisture-proof and will be damaged by wetness. Even if the walls are dry, install a film of polyethylene behind the furring strips to serve as a vapor barrier.

3 Pull the strip back off the wall and let it air for a few minutes (see panel adhesive label for time). This helps the adhesive dry more rapidly. Now press the furring strip into position once again, carefully centering it on the marked line. If you're applying furring to a conventional stud wall, locate the studs, then nail furring strips to the studs through the wall surface. To locate studs, use a stud finder, or drill holes near the base of the wall until you meet resistance. Mark the studs, then draw a plumb line over each.

4 Use a carpenter's level to plumb the first nailed strip as shown here. Each furring strip must be plumb to have good results. Double-check your 16-inch spacing as you proceed. Remember, solid backing is required along all four edges of each panel. If any adhesive adheres to your carpenter's level, wipe it off promptly with a rag and mineral spirits.

5 Using the level, check the remaining strips for plumb. Shingle shims slipped between the wall and the strips will help achieve a flat, uniform surface. Once you have a strip plumb, secure it to the wall with common nails (for wood frame walls) or with specially hardened masonry nails (for concrete or masonry walls). Drive the nail through the strip and shims into the wall. Nail into studs or mortar joints wherever possible. If you are working with masonry walls, use a baby sledge rather than a hammer.

6 Once you have the vertical furring strips in place, start on the horizontals. Measure between the verticals at top and bottom. Cut strips to fit at those locations between the verticals, allowing a ¼-inch gap for expansion. Apply adhesive, shim if necessary, and install. Fur completely around doors, windows, and other large openings. If you're installing board paneling in a diagonal, horizontal, or herringbone pattern, use the furring pattern just described. A vertical board installation requires more backing. Start at the floor and fur horizontally at 24-inch intervals; shim as needed.

INSTALLING PANELING
(continued)

Once your walls are ready and you've assembled all your tools and supplies, you'll be surprised at how quickly sheets of 4x8-foot paneling go up. You probably can do an entire room in a weekend. Take time, however, to make careful measurements and observe the manufacturer's recommendations. Follow the steps shown here to achieve a result you'll be proud of.

Allow paneling at least 48 hours to adjust to the room in which it will be installed. Ideally, you should stack panels with furring strips in alternating layers, permitting air to circulate freely. Like all wood, paneling responds to changes in temperature and humidity. Without this "adjustment period," the panels might expand or contract later, causing them to warp or crack.

Look for the best sequence

Part of the joy of working with wood products is their infinite variety. If your panels are veneered with wood, you'll never find two pieces exactly alike. Seize this advantage as you arrange panels on each wall.

Position the panels around the room as you think they'll go up, then shuffle them until you find the best combination of wood tones and grain patterns. Number the panels on the back in sequence, starting with the first corner panel.

Cutting and fastening

When you cut panels with a hand or table saw, place them faceup. When using a portable circular saw or sabre saw, cut facedown.

Apply paneling to walls with nails alone or with panel adhesive and nails. Grooves must fall over furring strips or studs at 16- or 24-inch intervals. Even apparently random-grooved paneling has grooves at these spacings. Nail into grooves wherever possible, using colored paneling nails. Countersink nail heads.

The drawings at *right* show how to apply sheet paneling over plaster or drywall surfaces, and the procedure is the same for installation over furring strips. To learn about putting up solid lumber, see pages 60 and 61. *(continued)*

PUTTING UP PANELS

1 The best place to start paneling is in a corner, and corners aren't always plumb. Slide a panel into the corner and plumb its outer edge as shown. Tack the panel in place. Holding the point and pencil of a compass parallel, follow the exact line of the corner from the ceiling to the floor. Guiding the point along the corner and the pencil down the panel edge will give you the corner's exact contour.

2 Take the panel down and trim along the scribed line. Test-fit in corner. Even if the corner isn't plumb, the panel will be. Before putting up the panels, mark the location of joints along each wall. Paint dark stripes on the wall where each joint will fall. This will hide the $\frac{1}{32}$-inch spacing you should allow between panels for expansion. Apply adhesive along the panel back as shown.

3 Align the first panel to the plumb line, then drive three or four color-matched nails halfway in along the top edge. Double-check the outside edge for plumb, and leave small spaces at the top and bottom. You can conceal these with crown molding at top and baseboard molding at bottom. If all checks out, compress the adhesive behind the panel by hammering the surface with a block of wood wrapped in cloth.

4 Pull the bottom of the panel away from the wall. Insert a piece of scrap about 4 to 5 inches wide to prop the panel away from the wall slightly. This helps the adhesive dry, ensuring a good bond. After three minutes, remove the scrap, press the panel to the wall, and drive nails every 8 inches along the edge and every 12 inches along intermediate grooves.

5 Continue paneling until you approach the next corner and need a cut-to-fit panel to finish the wall. Measure from the last panel you installed to the corner at several points along the panel edge. Then cut the next panel to fit.

6 To cut panels, use a crosscut hand saw with 10 teeth or more to the inch, a plywood blade in a table saw or circular saw, or a sabre saw. To minimize splintering, keep the saw sharp. If necessary, plane the edge of the panel to get as snug a fit as possible. Remember to maintain $\frac{1}{32}$-inch spacing between panel edges as you go.

7 Paneling around electrical outlets and heat registers requires careful measurements. Turn off the power to electrical outlets, unscrew the protective plate, and take horizontal dimensions from the edge of the last applied panel. Measure to the left and right edges of the outlet. The difference should be the outlet's width. Then measure from the floor to the top and bottom of outlet for height.

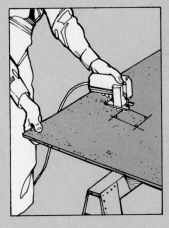

8 Transfer measurements to the panel, and double-check for accuracy. Outline the outlet shape on the panel face and drill ¾-inch starter holes at the four corners of the outline. Cut between the holes using a keyhole or sabre saw. You can cut the opening up to ¼ inch oversize and still cover it with the outlet plate.

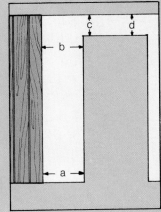

9 To panel around door or window openings, take measurements from the last panel installed. Measure from the floor or ceiling to find the height of the opening. Note the a, b, c, d sequence of measurements here. Try to lay out the panels so that their seams fall as near as possible to the center of the openings.

INSTALLING PANELING

(continued)

Solid board or strip paneling goes up in much the same way as sheet goods, but calls for much more cutting, fitting, and fastening. Solid stock offers a broader range of design choices. Boards can run horizontally, vertically, diagonally, or in a herringbone pattern, and their edges can be treated in a variety of ways. Here's how to achieve the effects you want.

Like sheet paneling, boards and strips need a couple of days to become acclimated to the moisture conditions in the room in which they'll be used. Spread out your lumber on the floor or against the wall for about 48 hours.

This also gives you a good chance to survey your stock. Note the different lengths, grain patterns, and colors and begin to arrange them for a random mix of natural variations. Cull any badly warped, knotted, or otherwise unsuitable pieces.

Nails or a combination of nails and paneling adhesive offers the best way to put up boards or strips. You have three choices:
• *Face-nailing,* or driving the nails straight through from front to back, as shown in steps 2 and 3 at *right.* If you want a rough look with nailheads showing, use 1½-inch common nails.
• *Countersinking* 1½-inch finishing nails with a nail set makes the nails much less obvious. For an even smoother appearance, fill nail holes with putty.
• *Blind-nailing* with 1½-inch finishing nails works with tongue-and-groove and shiplap boards. See steps 2 and 3 at *right.*

If you choose to use adhesive as well as nails, drive at least two nails at both the top and bottom of each board, more with extra-wide stock. Be sure to nail through plaster or drywall to the studs behind.

If you're using tongue-and-groove lumber, the last course in a corner (with vertical paneling) or at the floor or ceiling (with horizontal paneling) can be difficult to install. If you bevel the underside of the final edge, the last board will snap snugly into place.

DIAGONAL BOARDS

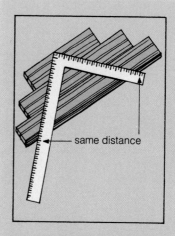

same distance

1 Diagonal and other special patterns aren't difficult once you know how to achieve them. Start in an inside corner. Locate studs and mark with vertical lines. Place the first three boards together on the floor. Butt edges tightly, then put a carpenter's square over the boards and mark across all three for 45-degree miter cuts as shown.

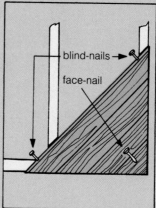

blind-nails

face-nail

2 Make the cuts and trial-fit the boards into the corner. If they have tongues, the tongues should face up. If the boards don't fit, your corner is probably out of plumb and you'll have to mark angles with a bevel gauge, as shown in drawing 5.

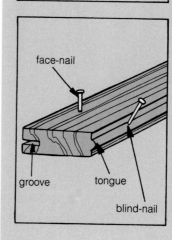

face-nail

groove   tongue

blind-nail

3 Now you are ready to face-nail the first plank in place in the corner. If you are using tongue-and-groove boards, blind-nail the rest of the planking at each end and at intersecting studs or furring strips. If you countersink these nails, the groove in the next board will interlock snugly.

4 Measure lengths from outside edges of preceding boards. When you transfer measurements and mark the 45-degree miter cuts, orient the new board parallel to the wall so you can check whether your miters will run in the right direction. Even pros miscut miters occasionally.

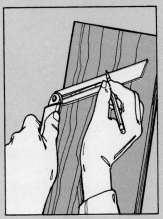

5 Not all floors and ceilings are perfectly level, and not all corners are truly plumb. If your wall is out of square, 45-degree miters won't work. Adjust a bevel gauge to fit the true angle, tighten its pivot screw, then transfer to the new board as shown. This simple device marks absolutely accurate angles every time.

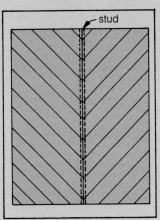

6 A chevron or herringbone pattern calls for careful measuring and fitting. Cut 45-degree miters on the board or strip ends that will butt together. Read angles at the floor and ceiling with a bevel gauge. Align the 45-degree miters over the center of a stud or a furring strip that you know is perfectly plumb.

EDGE TREATMENTS

What you do with edge joints offers a way to add texture to a wall paneled with solid lumber. Simple butt joints and tongue-and-groove joints result in a relatively flat surface compared to the effects you can achieve with these special joint treatments.

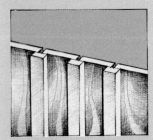

Board-and-batten
Wide boards go on the wall first with narrow, even gaps between them. Batten strips cover the gaps, giving the wall surface a bold, three-dimensional look.

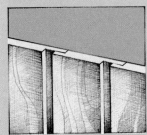

Shiplap
For this effect, you need specially milled boards with a wide rabbet along one edge, a narrower reverse rabbet along the other. Interlocking shiplap edges creates a "negative" board-and-batten effect.

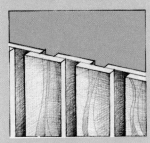

Board-on-board
This texture produces a weightier effect than any of the other treatments. It's similar to board-and-batten, but the battens are identical to the boards. Board-on-board requires only slightly more material because the gaps are wider.

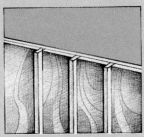

Strip facing
Also similar to board-and-batten, this texture offers a more subtle, reserved effect. Background boards are spaced only wide enough to accommodate 1½-inch-wide strips. The strips project ¾ inch from the boards.

METAL AND MIRRORS

In the mood for something bright and shiny? If you are, try waking up your walls with metal or mirrors. Most of us don't readily think of metal as an interior surface, which is why it can be a big attention-getter. Mirrors brighten walls and visually multiply space. The more you put up, the more dazzle and dimension you can create. Here's a survey of the ways metal and mirrors can add sparkle to the scene at your house.

G linting corrugated walls, *above,* tempt you to reach out and touch. Usually you find aluminum panels like these out in the country on pole barns or storage sheds. Here an imaginative homeowner brought them indoors to cover some badly cracked walls.

You can purchase similar panels at building supply stores in standard widths of 26 and 48 inches and lengths of 8, 10, or 12 feet. To install corrugated metal, first attach furring strips to the wall (see pages 56 and 57). Panel

edges are designed to overlap and often are predrilled so you can nail through two edges at once. Secure with special ring-type nails designed for use with corrugated metal.

Metal of 20-gauge thickness or less cuts easily with sheet metal snips, and you can file edges for snug fits around doors, windows, and other irregularities.

Aluminum and galvanized steel paneling are inexpensive.

In a few areas, such as near a wood stove, you might prefer the mellow warmth of copper or the cool elegance of brushed stainless steel. Although much more costly, these metals offer a smooth, noncorrugated look.

Oldtime "tin"—a ceiling material that works on walls

Remember the ornate metal ceilings in turn-of-the-century buildings? Decorative pressed-metal panels are back in style and available again in original patterns stamped out of light-weight sheet metal. This material comes in 2x6-foot or 2x8-foot panels that install on walls or on ceilings.

First put up furring strips in 2x6- or 2x8-foot grids, then nail strips to the furring. Interlocking nipples along edges assure correct alignment when you overlap panels. Trim with matching pressed-metal moldings if you like. (More about pressed metal on pages 88 and 89.)

Mirrors, mirrors, mirrors
The headboard treatment at *right* illustrates how mirrors can brighten and enlarge almost any room. With mirrored walls, a small space goes from cramped to comfortable. Tight quarters such as halls or dining areas gain depth.

Order plate mirrors cut to size and install with mirror adhesive and special steel clips sold at glass outlets. If you're concerned about cracking a mirror, many firms will install it for you.

An alternative is mirror tiles, 1- and 2-foot squares that go up like ceramic tile (see pages 70 and 71). Although more expensive than equivalent areas of plate mirror, tiles are easier to work with.

Mirror walls are durable and easy to keep clean, but don't locate one where close traffic will produce daily smudges and smears.

EXPOSING
BRICK

Like wood, brick has earned lots of honors over the years. It's honest, never seems out of style, and can last a lifetime without maintenance. If yours is an older home with solid brick walls, there might be treasure hidden behind crumbling plaster. Exposing brick is messy, arduous, and monotonous work, but once it is done, you will be rewarded with a wall you can be proud of. (If you live in a newer home with little or no brick, don't give up hope. Brick veneers can go up almost anywhere. Pages 66 and 67 tell about veneering with brick.)

It's hard to know what you might find behind old walls, which makes exposing brick a bit like prospecting. Just as a prospector pans for gold before starting a mine, you'll want to chip away an inconspicuous section to see what's back there.

Hit the wall with a hammer or crowbar until chunks of plaster crack and begin to fall, then pry them away. Was the plaster applied directly to brick? If it was, you'll have to do more cleaning than if furring strips and lath were put up first.

Scrub the brick vigorously with a wire brush to remove plaster residue or dirt. Do you like the color? Are mortar joints crumbling and in need of repair? In the home *opposite*, the discovery of handmade bricks in rich earth tones, interspersed with rough-textured mortar joints, spurred on the demolition work. No two bricks look quite the same. If you don't like the color of the bricks you find, paint them for an effect like the cool, whitewashed wall at *right*.

Let the dust fly
If you like what you see and decide to bring it out into the open, prepare for some dusty, time-consuming work. Clear all furnishings out of the room and drape openings with plastic sheeting. Protect flooring with plastic.

Don a hardhat, heavy clothing, work gloves, goggles, and a dust mask. If the plaster is backed by lath and furring strips, you probably can break it loose with a heavy wrecking bar and pry the furring from the brick. You may need a sledge hammer to break loose plaster that was applied directly to brick.

It doesn't take long to get plaster down. Shoveling it, hauling it away, and cleaning residue from the brick are other matters. Plaster is heavy, so plan to remove debris in small boxes. Most municipal garbage services won't handle construction trash, so you'll probably have to take the plaster to a dump yourself.

Cleaning and sealing
With a hand- or power-operated wire brush, go over the entire surface to remove solid residue. Powder that remains in pores of the brick and mortar can be washed away with a 40 to 60 percent solution of muriatic acid. (You'll need a breathing mask and other protective gear for both jobs.)

After washing with acid, rinse well with clear water and let the bricks dry for a day or two. Seal them by brushing or spraying with polyurethane. If you neglect to seal bricks, lime dust will work its way to the surface. Polyurethane deepens and enriches brick colors, yet soaks in to give a matte finish. If you want a shinier surface, apply another coat or two.

VENEERING WITH BRICK

If you're not blessed with an original wall of well-aged bricks or stonework, how can you re-create the colonial aura of a New England cottage or the old Chicago look of a restored townhouse? Brick veneer is the answer.

We're not talking about those phony-looking sheets of stamped plastic you may have seen. Brick and stone veneers look like brick and stone because they are thin slices of the real thing. Produced in many styles, colors, textures, and shapes, brick and stone veneers can give any wall the permanent look of masonry.

If there is one room in the house where an easy-care surface is worth a lot of elbow grease, it's the kitchen. Kitchen walls need good looks and easy maintenance. In the kitchen *above,* a mixture of textures and colors combines rich wood tones, lush green-ery, sleek counter tops, and metal cookware with the traditional warmth of old brick.

The result is eminently inviting, a workplace that lures family and friends, yet minimizes housekeeping. Brick- and stone-veneered products are also fireproof, making them ideal for use near a fireplace, wood stove, or kitchen appliances.

Appearance options include square and irregularly cut shapes, smooth, medium, and heavily textured surfaces, and colors that range from bright

PUTTING UP BRICK VENEER

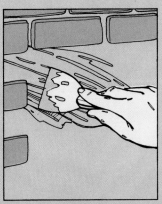

1 Before you can veneer with masonry, you must prepare the wall surface. Wipe off dust and grease, and remove any wallpaper. Then apply the adhesive mortar, starting with a thin coat (about $1/16$ inch) on a 2x4-foot section. Put up some brick and continue working in small wall sections, adding adhesive as you go.

2 Mount bricks from the top down, working to the right. Finish two rows at a time, then work your way down the left side. Place each brick in the mortar firmly, and wiggle a bit to set in place. Allow $3/8$-inch spacing between bricks for mortar lines. At doors, windows, and corners use a hacksaw to cut bricks to fit. Dress up edges with a file.

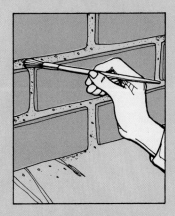

3 Using a narrow brush, smooth adhesive into the space between joints to form mortar lines. Also cover joint lines at the base. Stroke slowly and smoothly to ensure an even thickness. Wipe off excess mortar before it dries. Smoothing mortar between tiles makes joints easier to clean.

4 Finish off the wall with a coat of non-glossy sealer. One coat will suffice unless your new surface will be subject to grease or water splattering. If so, you may need one or two coats more. Well-sealed surfaces wash clean with warm water and mild detergent. Dry them with a damp sponge.

---

white and red to rich earth tones. For a variegated look, mix several brick veneers.

Easy to put up
If you examine the drawings above, you can see that lightweight brick and stone veneers are easy to install, even for a beginning do-it-yourselfer. Their appearance mimics old, heavy masonry, yet you can put them up without calling in an expensive installer or undertaking special shoring or foundation work.

Whether you're remodeling or building, you'll find this product relatively inexpensive and unusually versatile. Brick lends itself to contemporary and high-tech styling, yet its down-home warmth complements country, traditional, or south-of-the-border furnishings. Brick's texture and tone contrast with natural materials like wood and wicker, and with accessories in brass, chrome, or plastics.

Wall make-ready
The flat, tilelike bricks come in cartons and can be installed with an adhesive mortar. The tools you need are a hacksaw, file, narrow brush, and trowel. Brick-veneered and stone-veneered wall coverings can be applied to any type of rigid, nonflaking surface, including plaster, plywood, cement, cement block, drywall, brick, concrete, or asbestos board. Follow the manufacturer's instructions and take your time to ensure a handsome result.

Once it is in place, you'll have a highly durable wall that should bring years of low-maintenance service. To clean, wash with warm water and a mild detergent; dry with a damp sponge.

CERAMIC TILE

Ceramic tile has been around a long time. Centuries-old installations in ancient Persia still look lustrous today. Because tile has a high tolerance for abuse, it holds up well even in heavily trafficked public spaces such as New York subway stations. Despite their permanence, ceramic tiles are only moderately difficult to install. If you master the procedures shown on pages 70 and 71, you'll be well on your way to a successful tile project. But first let's look at the properties of this material and the ways it can be used.

Ceramic tile deserves its reputation as a waterproof wall covering par excellence, but tile offers even more advantages: It is fireproof, durable, and a breeze to clean.

Ceramic tile begins life as a natural, earth-born material—clay. Fired in high-temperature kilns, tile will not dent, warp, peel, or fade. Although it is relatively brittle, once tile is cemented to a solid backing and joints are grouted with mortar, it makes a strong and long-lasting surface. Hot pans, greasy splatters, and sticky fingers don't faze it.

Tile is available in a wide choice of textures, patterns, colors, shapes, and sizes. Imports from France, Italy, Mexico, and elsewhere compete with American-made selections. Prices range from moderate to expensive. Specialty items, such as vivid colors, cost up to two or three times more than standard tiles. Ceramic tile isn't cheap, but you can safely consider it an investment that calls for almost no maintenance and one that lasts practically forever.

Tile's many moods
Foyers, kitchens, baths, and solariums are obvious candidates for ceramic tile wall treatments. In tandem with tiled counters, floors, and benches, tiled walls can wrap from one surface to the next in complementary or monochromatic colors.

The kitchen *above* features a provincial motif in glazed 4x4-inch ceramic tiles applied to the counter, backsplash, and range hood. Here a balanced placement of solid-color and decorated tiles contributes to a country look, but you are just as likely to find tile in sleek contemporary, art nouveau, or quietly traditional settings.

In the bath at *right,* the mood is sophisticated and slightly Moorish. Framed in warm beige-tone tiles, intricately patterned coral tiles add visual texture. This restrained ornamental pattern on the floor, counter top, and shower wall makes the small room appear larger. The reverse treatment—a decorative border around plain tiles—works equally well.

Glazes and textures

From great bold quarry tiles to tiny, smooth mosaics, the ceramic variations are endless. Fired with brilliant colors and glazes, or earth-toned and somber, tiles encompass the primitive and sophisticated, the cool and the daring.

Unglazed tile has a matte surface; glazes can have either matte or shiny finishes. Smooth, flat, granular, or softly sculptured surfaces are other options. Porcelain ceramic tiles offer a fine-grained body.

Tile care

Ceramic tiles will not scorch, burn, or blister, and they repel water. They need only routine cleaning with mild detergent. Grease and food stains are wiped off glazed tiles with soap and water, but unglazed quarry tiles are subject to staining by grease and oil. Unglazed tiles resist scratching in areas where you don't want a slick surface; glazed tiles eventually show scratch marks. Porcelain ceramic tile offers an impervious surface both indoors and out, and is stainproof, dentproof, even frostproof. Silicone sealer applied to grouting between the tiles keeps it stain-free. *(continued)*

CERAMIC TILE
(continued)

A typical ceramic tile installation requires two types of tile: *field tiles* to cover most of the surface and *trim tiles* to round the edges and turn corners.

Sold by the linear foot, trim tiles, although necessary, are expensive additions. These special tiles come in many configurations, including cap pieces, bullnose, round and straight cove, runners, out-angles, and miter corners.

Field tiles come in 4¼-, 6-, and 8-inch squares, in small and large hexagonals, and in oblong shapes. Wall tiles are ¼ inch to $\frac{5}{16}$ inch thick, depending on type. Small mosaic tiles come bonded to pieces of 1x1-foot or 1x2-foot paper or fabric mesh. Mosaic tiles are 1x1-, 1x2-, or 2x2-inch pieces. They can be installed faster than individual tiles but require more grout.

Pregrouted tile sheets include 4¼-inch tiles and flexible synthetic grouting. All you do is cement the sheets to the wall and seal edges with a caulking gun. Although they are easiest to install, pregrouted tiles include only a limited range of colors and styles.

Professional installers usually prefer to "mud-set" ceramic tiles in cement-base mortar, a difficult masonry job for the amateur. Most do-it-yourselfers find it easier to use any of several mastic-like adhesives. Consult with your dealer for a recommendation.

Tools for tiling

A *tile cutter* makes quick, accurate, and straight lines. *Glass cutters* work too, but more slowly. *Nippers* nibble out curved pieces.

A *notched trowel's* serrated edges spread adhesive to the proper thickness; a *notched spreader* works better in tight places.

Grouting usually is done with a *rubber float*, but a window washer's squeegee also works.

Practice cutting a few tiles to get the hang of it. You can rent cutters and nippers from many tile dealers.

Preparing walls for tile

Apply tile to plywood, drywall, or plaster walls as long as the walls are smooth, sound, and firm. Strip flexible wall coverings such as wallpaper, and scrape any loose paint. Lightly sand glossy surfaces.

Seal new drywall with a thin coat of adhesive, packing openings where pipes come through. Don't bother to tape or smooth drywall joints. You should always install water-resistant drywall or exterior-grade plywood in high-moisture areas such as showers.

Take extra care to chip away old material where tile meets the top of the tub or shower; leave ¼ inch of space. After tiling, apply caulk.

Now you're ready to begin laying out the job. Start with the first tile in the center on the next-to-bottom row, and proceed toward the edges to get tiles that are cut to the same width in both corners. Or, if that's not important to you, start in a corner. But check for plumb first. Some tiles along the edges probably will need trimming to compensate for a slightly off-square surface.

PUTTING UP TILES

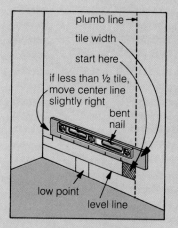

plumb line
tile width
start here
if less than ½ tile, move center line slightly right
bent nail
low point
level line

1 Fasten a level to a board you know is straight. On the board mark off tile widths, including $\frac{1}{16}$-inch grouting. Mark a plumb line at the wall's midpoint and use the board as a guide to see how tiles will fall at the edges. Shift the field if necessary. Mark a level line one tile-width above the wall's lowest point. Begin setting full-size tiles just above this line. If you are tiling a backsplash or tub, begin with the bottom row.

2 Apply adhesive in 2- to 3-foot sections. Maintain good ventilation to disperse fumes. Spread the adhesive with the trowel's notched edge; comb it out in beaded lines. The spaces between lines should be almost free of adhesive. Set the first tiles in place using a slight twisting motion, but don't slide them. Leave $\frac{1}{16}$-inch spaces between tiles for grout.

3 Check each tile for proper spacing to be sure it is square with adjoining tiles. Press it firmly into the adhesive. If adhesive oozes from beneath the tile, you have applied too much. Use a toothpick to remove the excess before it dries, then try spreading the adhesive more thinly.

4 To trim tiles with a tile cutter, apply firm pressure and score a single, even line. Snap the tile with a flick of the handle. With a glass cutter, use a carpenter's square as a guide. Score the tile only once; rescoring results in ragged breaks. Place the score over an edge and snap downward. Smooth edges with a file or abrasive stone. Also use a file to enlarge holes or cut notches.

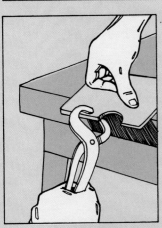

5 Use tile nippers or a pair of regular pliers to make curved cuts or to pinch thin slivers off the side. You can avoid breaking the tile by starting at the edge and taking small bites at a time. Fit tiles to a tub or other curved fixture by scribing with a compass. Let the steel point follow the fixture's contour while the compass's pencil or pen marks the tile; then cut.

6 To fit tiles around pipes or other obstructions, drill through with a masonry bit or piece in a trimmed tile. Measure the opening and mark on tile. Cut the tile in half along the pipe's center axis and nibble out semicircular notches on each piece. Don't worry about precise accuracy, because standard plates for plumbing and electrical fixtures will cover small flaws.

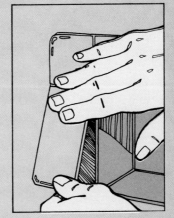

7 Install soap dishes and other ceramic accessories last. Cement them in place with adhesive or two-part epoxy putty. Use masking tape to hold the accessories in place until the putty dries. Don't apply pressure for a week or so. Press trim pieces in place after you've finished laying out the other tiles.

8 Mix grout to the consistency of thick paste and apply it over the tile with diagonal swipes of the rubber float. Be sure to pack it in all joints. Wait 10 to 15 minutes, then shape joints with a rounded object such as a toothbrush handle. This helps to compact the grout.

9 Now wash all grout off tiles with a wet sponge. Finally, polish with a soft, dry cloth. Don't use a newly tiled shower during the curing period of about two weeks. Apply a silicone sealer to protect the grout.

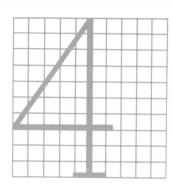

EXPRESS YOURSELF WITH ART

Art brings instant impact and appeal to any room. Whether your taste (and budget) run to one-of-a-kind paintings, one-of-a-series prints, drawings, watercolors, or mass-produced posters, what you put on your walls can express your personality as clearly as the clothes you wear. If you're a newcomer to the art world, fear not. This chapter surveys your main choices, tells how to select a suitable frame, and explains how to display your art to its best advantage.

Art has many definitions, but in the final analysis, it can be *anything* you happen to like. It may be a painting, a photograph, a grouping of folk art checkerboards, Grandma's quilt, or kids' watercolors. The point is this: What you hang on your walls should be personal, something that delights you, has special meaning, or says something about your tastes and interests. Simply "filling space" is not enough.

If you're not sure what kind of art you like, look in museums, galleries, and books to see what techniques, subjects, and colors appeal to you. In the dining room at *right,* for example, the homeowner selected crisp black and white prints to add drama and pattern. A few select furnishings, neutral carpet, and white walls create a simple backdrop that focuses attention on the artwork.

If you're tired of your blank walls but not ready to buy art, rent a piece from a rental gallery or museum gift shop, or buy a poster or two. (Try mail-order catalogs, galleries, or local theater, symphony, or historical preservation groups, which often use posters to advertise their events.) Priced from about $10 to $35 apiece, posters often are high-quality lithographs or silk screens, artwork you can afford now. Affordable art will buy time to select "the real thing."

(continued)

SELECTING ART
(continued)

Art is so varied, you can choose among items that will suit almost any taste or budget. When you learn something about the different forms art can take, you will be on your way to one of the joys of collecting: developing your own "eye." Here are four main categories of artworks.

Paintings

Oils, acrylics, and other one-of-a-kind images usually demand a great deal of an artist's time and talent, and often require expensive materials. They tend to be the most costly wall-hung artworks, especially those by well-known artists.

Most of us will never own an original Rembrandt oil or Calder gouache, but works by local and regional artists can be surprisingly affordable. What's more, by staying close to home you may have an opportunity to meet the artists, and perhaps visit their studios. Knowing the person who created a work makes it more meaningful.

Some artists sell their works directly at shows or by appointment. Others are represented by galleries. Reputable art dealers protect both artists and collectors by assuring that the artist receives a fair price for the work, and by warranting that the buyer is purchasing an original piece. Beware of so-called "dealers" who operate on a sidewalk, from a van, or in a motel room. Their wares are often cheap reproductions or paintings done by hired hands in a factory-like setting.

Watercolors, drawings, and other paper works

Not all original art commands the high prices that paintings on canvas or wood do. Water-colors, drawings, pastels, charcoals, and other paper works often require less time to produce. That means you may be able to buy a fine paper work from a well-known artist for the same price as an oil or acrylic from a less famous painter, or pay a modest price for a decent work by an artist who is not in the spotlight.

Prints

Printmaking has come into its own as a fine art form. An original print is not the same thing as a photomechanical copy of an oil painting or other work. A photomechanical print is merely a reproduction of a work that originally was done in another medium.

On the other hand, when an artist sets out to create a series of limited-edition prints, he or she makes a master image on a metal or plastic plate, stone, wood block, or silk screen. The image then is transferred to paper. After the artist signs the resulting prints and numbers them, the master image is destroyed or defaced. The paper print *is* the work of art, and that master image was only the means to achieve it.

Editions range from 25 to 500, and each print is numbered. The mark 5/30, for example, tells that the print was number five in an edition of 30.

Among the most popular types of printmaking are: relief (woodcuts), intaglio (etchings), lithographs (made by chemical printing), and serigraphs (a silk-screen process).

In *relief* printing, the artist uses a knife or other tool to cut an image into linoleum or wood. To produce the print, the artist inks the wood or linoleum block. The lines and sections that were cut away remain unprinted, while the ink adheres to the raised surface to produce the image.

The detail in an *intaglio* print (etching) will be finer and more delicate than in a relief print. The artist meticulously etches the design into a metal plate (usually a copper alloy). To make the print, the artist forces a thick ink into the scratches of the plate, then wipes the surface. The paper is placed over the plate and a wringer applies enough pressure to force the ink out of the crevasses onto the paper.

In another intaglio method, a metal plate is coated with a substance that resists acid. Then the artist etches the design into the surface, removing the coating and exposing the plate's surface. The plate is placed in an acid bath where the etched-out designs are eaten away, leaving sunken areas into which the ink is forced.

An intaglio print is made on damp paper using heavy pressure, so you should be able to see an embossment or plate mark on the paper.

A *lithograph* is produced from a planographic method in which the master image is done on a flat surface. A lithograph resembles a brush or crayon drawing.

To produce a lithograph, the artist uses grease ink (called tusche) to draw on a prepared limestone block or zinc plate. The block or plate then is chemically treated so the greased areas attract the ink while the rest of the paper repels it. The inked stone and damp paper are passed through a press that squeezes the ink onto the paper. Most artists continue to use a slow, centuries-old printing method that involves hand-inking and printing each print individually, but some use machine printing, which prints many times faster but often with lower quality. Know which type you are buying.

Unlike the crayon-drawing method of lithography, a *serigraph* is produced by a silk-screening method much like a stencil. Ink remains on the surface of the paper instead of being absorbed. Many fabrics are printed this way.

To make a serigraph, the artist uses a stretched screen of silk (sometimes nylon), then blocks the areas not to be printed by applying a varnish or paper pattern to the screen. Ink is pressed through those parts of the screen that are not blocked out. The resulting image is not reversed, as in a lithograph, but is exactly what passes through the screen.

Folk art

"Folk art" was the art of the common man. Before the camera and mass-produced print came into use, the folk-art painters traveled the country, hiring themselves out to capture the faces and places of their time. These itinerant painters chronicled social events, glimpses into everyday living, and the faces of their patrons. Today, folk-art paintings are valued for their history and for their almost childlike disregard for perspective and reality. Some folk-art paintings were oil-on-wood creations, others were created in oil or watercolor on velvet, paper, or silk. Two of the folk-art portraits *opposite* typify this simple style.

A word of caution: Some dealers (and even collectors) will stress the idea of buying art for investment. At best, such investment buying is tricky for the amateur. While your purchase may, in fact, rise in value over the years, it's best to buy art because you like it.

FRAMING

Displaying your artwork effectively first means framing it. The primary function of the frame is not decorative. It should protect the artwork from damage caused by handling or exposure to the environment. You want to prolong the life of the work by protecting it from dirt, grease, air pollutants, and environmental changes, such as high humidity and the harsh dryness of furnace heat. Only after protection is assured should you be concerned about a frame's decorative properties.

Your artwork purchase can be damaged by improper or too-frequent handling, by framing or matting with the wrong materials, and by hanging in an unsafe place in your home.

Paintings

Glass is usually not used to cover the surface of oils and acrylics because it tends to attract moisture, which can lead to mildew and other problems. But a frame around the edges of a stretched canvas protects the painting from unnecessary handling. If a work is especially large and hangs almost to the floor, an extra-deep frame can recess it enough to protect the work from the nicks and cracked pigment caused by accidental blows from passers-by and cleaning equipment.

Prints

Works of art on paper present other problems. Unless acid-free materials are used in mounting and matting the work, damage can occur. Rusty blotches called "foxing" result from acid present in regular cardboard backing.

In addition, the condensation of moisture on the glass can cause stains and destroy colors. The top edges of the print should be attached to its acid-free mounting only with acid-free materials, such as linen-tape hinges or hinges made from rice paper and wheat paste. Under no circumstances should the work be glued down. The paper needs room to expand and contract.

A mat is important, acting as a buffer between the work of art and the glass. (If no mat is desired, you can "float" your print on a rag board backing, using metal or wood fillets along the inside edges of the frame to keep the paper away from the glass.)

Glass often is used to protect prints, but acrylic is another possibility. It does not attract condensation as easily as glass, it resists shattering, and it filters out some harmful light. Because acrylic is lightweight, it often is preferred for large works.

One caution: Acrylic tends to produce static electricity, which not only attracts dust and dirt, but also can pull parts of a charcoal or pastel image from the paper.

Non-glare glass can be used over some items, but it is best avoided on fine art because it tends to flatten colors.

Decorative framing

Beautifully framed art can create a mood, inspire a color scheme, serve as a decorative accent, even direct the eye toward (or away from) an architectural detail. The frame should never be more important than the artwork.

What can you do for your artwork with frames and mats? You can change the impact of each piece or change the impact of a grouping by varying or matching the frames and mats. A larger mat, for instance, can give greater visual impact to a small print.

In the room *opposite*, groups of items have been unified in three ways: by matching frames, by matching sizes and colors of mats, and by subject matter. If such symmetry and uniformity are not what you want, you might try varying the mat sizes to change the dimensions of each piece.

Custom framing

In most cases, custom framing is your best framing option, although probably the most expensive. Always specify acid-free materials when framing a prized piece of artwork.

A professional frame shop probably will have a larger selection of frames, matting, and materials than you can find elsewhere. Shop personnel will be able to help you select a frame to protect the art and complement it aesthetically. In such a shop, your frame will be made to the desired measurements and your matting will be cut by hand to fit the print. Frame corners will be glued, nailed, and hand-finished, and mitered corners will be sealed.

To find a good framer, ask other collectors, artists, and personnel at galleries.

Ready-made frames

A ready-made frame comes complete with glass, stapled fitting devices, a backing, and a hanger. It will save you money on items not considered valuable.

Another option for less valuable art is the "fast frame," four clamp-on corners or strips for the top and bottom of the art. Plastic clips hold glass and backing board together like a sandwich.

Do-it-yourself frames

If you have steady hands, patience, and the proper tools, you can make your own frames. Books or local adult education classes tell you how.

DISPLAYING ART

After you find and frame your treasures, it's time to hang them so you can sit back and enjoy them. A grouping of small items or the presence of one large piece can become the focal point for any room. As you see in the rooms on these pages, there are few rules to inhibit you. A grouping can be hung formally (with matched frames and mats and symmetrical placement) or in a collection where frames and mats vary and informal balance prevails. Here are guidelines.

If you have several smaller items or an especially large wall you want to take advantage of, an arrangement of artwork pieces may be your best bet. Such an assemblage can give decorative impact to small pieces that might be lost visually if displayed separately.

In groupings, artwork can be keyed by color, subject matter, or by matching frames and mats. But for interest, consider varying sizes and shapes of items in an arrangement. Another way to add variety is by varying frame depths.

To keep a grouping from looking disorderly, create a geometric shape with the outer edges of the grouping and plan for at least one or two straight lines to run through the arrangement.

You can achieve cohesiveness by hanging items relatively close together so they appear to be a unit. Make sure that one item in an arrangement doesn't overshadow the others. For example, a delicate watercolor can be overwhelmed if hung next to strong oils or posters.

To plan a grouping, lay the pieces on the floor and arrange and rearrange them until you come up with an eye-pleasing combination. For informal groupings, balance one large item at one end with smaller pieces at the other.

Backgrounds

Whether you're hanging an arrangement or a single item, consider your backgrounds. A strongly patterned wall, for example, may clash with the work of art (or make it virtually disappear). To create "breathing space" that will separate artwork from a patterned wall, choose wide, solid-color mats and frames. If you choose a painted wall, plain white can be an effective backdrop, but you may be surprised at how well a dark-painted wall can showcase art. For example, imagine how distinctively mellow old black-and-white etchings would stand out against a dark-brown wall.

How high?

Artwork is best hung at "eye level," but the meaning of that term varies. Decide whether the artwork will most often be viewed while standing or sitting, consider the space as a whole, and then decide how high to hang the work.

(continued)

DISPLAYING ART

(continued)

One of the delights of owning artwork is arranging and rearranging pieces as your mood changes. Sometimes a piece or an arrangement that has been in the same place for months or years loses its impact because you are accustomed to seeing it there. You may be surprised at how your perception will be changed if you hang the art in another spot.

Although you probably don't want to treat your artwork as "wallpaper" by slavishly matching it to your decor, you do want it to blend with your decorating scheme. You can tie the artwork into your room scheme by adding an accessory or two to repeat the artwork colors, or you can pick up imagery from the art itself.

Altering space

The way you hang your artwork can change your perception of space in your home in dramatic ways. You can use artwork to direct the eye. In a room with a cathedral ceiling, for example, hanging a large painting or arrangement higher than usual will direct the eye upward. Conversely, hanging artwork lower than usual can bring about a feeling of coziness and play down a ceiling that is too high.

Take a look at the room shown *above.* The poster turns a corner, making the corner virtually disappear.

If you have a narrow room, hanging a grouping of items straight across the narrow end wall will produce an illusion of width. If you have a low ceiling, a narrow vertical grouping reaching almost to the ceiling will create a feeling of height.

Going "solo"

An especially large or fine work of art may demand

space around it to be appreciated. Don't feel that you must fill every empty expanse of wall. By hanging a treasured piece alone on a wall, as shown *opposite,* you let the work assume the center-stage position it deserves. (Avoid hanging a painting above a fireplace mantel, where it might be damaged by heat or smoke or acquire a coat of soot.)

Lighting

Although you want to illuminate your artwork effectively, avoid hanging artwork in direct sunlight for long. The light can damage the paper, dry the oils, and fade the colors.

Here are a few lighting tips. First, avoid placing incandescent lights so close to artwork that their heat causes damage. Unfiltered fluorescent or ultraviolet light can damage colors.

(Prints, oils, watercolors, and pastels are especially vulnerable to damage from strong light; some acrylics are less susceptible.)

For large items hung close to the floor, simple plug-in uplights can be effective. Items on or near shelves can be lighted with clamp-on spotlights or miniature track lights.

For other wall items, track lighting is the most flexible option. (More on track lights on pages 92 and 93.) You can use wall-washer track fixtures to light a large grouping, or use spotlights to highlight each piece individually.

Varying the type of bulb in a fixture lets you use different types of light for different works. For example, a wide-beam flood lamp can illuminate a large work, and you can later substitute spotlights

or flood lamps with different beam spreads to change the configuration of the light beam. If you're considering installing a track system, consider low-voltage lights. They save energy and produce a narrow beam of intense light to illuminate small objects without spilling unwanted light onto adjacent surfaces.

With any track lights, aim for about a 45-degree beam angle. Try to illuminate the object without bouncing light into the eyes of persons seated or walking through the space.

Cove lighting is another option. Installed on the room's perimeter or along a wall, cove lighting washes artwork with soft light. Traditional plug-in picture lights, which clamp to the frame, work for oils and acrylics but produce glare on artwork covered with glass.

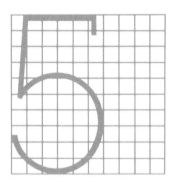

5
MAKE YOUR CEILINGS SPECIAL

The easiest thing to do with a ceiling is to paint it white and forget it, and in most instances that's the best policy, too. But when a room needs more than emptiness overhead, you want a ceiling to star in its own right. This chapter explores ways to groom your ceiling for a major role, starting with paint.

WITH PAINT

When you walk into the room shown here, your eyes look up first, then they move down to take in the rest of the scene. Unexpected color on the ceiling and crown molding around it create a visual magnet. Continuing the same color down the window frame guides your attention to contemporary furnishings that would have been lost in an all-white room.

Accenting a ceiling with paint can make a high ceiling seem lower, a narrow room wider, a dull room brighter. On the other hand, paint's power can be easily misused, especially on ceilings. Before you rush off to a paint store, consider these important principles, then choose your colors accordingly.

• Dark, intense colors work only on unusually high ceilings of 10 feet or more. On lower ceilings deep tones absorb too much light, making a room dim and oppressive.

• A vivid color can wake up a room, but it can also be overpowering. Proceed carefully, paying attention to the decor in the rest of the room. A rich melon color works for this ceiling because it doesn't compete with the neutral tones of the upholstery, tables, and floor.

• Light pastels such as sky blue or sunny yellow can raise a ceiling, especially if the walls are painted a deeper shade of the same color.

• Even bright, pure white can be tricky in a room with colored walls because it will pick up a reflection of the wall colors. If reflections bother you, paint the ceiling off-white.

MAKE YOUR CEILINGS SPECIAL

WITH FABRIC, VINYL, AND PAPER

The decorative impact of paper, vinyl, or fabric can wake up any surface, and that goes double for problem ceilings with odd angles and shapes. Turn those angles to advantage by accenting them. The results are just as gratifying on ordinary ceilings. You can give a room pattern and texture, cover a blemished surface, emphasize architectural features, or make up for a lack of them. Putting up ceiling coverings, however, is not a job for novice paperhangers. If you've never worked with wall coverings before, start with walls and work your way up, or call in a professional to do the job.

Crisp checked fabric makes something special of a dropped ceiling in the family room at *right*. Bending around inside and outside corners, the pattern sets off white walls and dark wood molding.

Sections of fabric were stitched together and stapled to the ceiling. Navy gimp covers the staples and defines the edges.

You could achieve the same look with paper or vinyl wall coverings. However, avoid large-scale patterns or strong contrasting colors. They tend to overpower the room, hanging overhead like a threatening weight.

Small-scale, subdued patterns will produce almost the same effect as a solid color. For best results, select a matte-finish, fabric-backed vinyl wall covering. Avoid glossy foils because they emphasize surface irregularities.

Hang paper or vinyl across the width of the room, starting above the most prominent wall or opposite the doorway. On the ceiling, mark a chalk line parallel to the wall and use it as a guide for your first strip. Plan ahead so you don't have to split the final strip to make it fit. If necessary, you can overlap the middle sections slightly.

Upholstering a ceiling
To make a ceiling warm and handsome, "slip-cover" it. In the attic bedroom *opposite*, channel-quilted cotton duck was applied over ¼ inch of foam. The result: a hushed, muffled, and intimate bedroom atmosphere.

If you decide to upholster a ceiling or wall, choose wide fabric or king-size sheets. Minimizing the number of seams makes the job easier.

Hang the first panel along a line you know is true. Use pushpins, double-face tape, or a helper to hold the panels. Staple the first panel to the wall or ceiling surface. Trim or turn under at ceiling edges, baseboards, corners, or window frames.

To hide staples where two panels meet, make a concealed seam. Place the second panel facedown on the first and match patterns at the seam. Staple the seam through both thicknesses, then staple a strip of upholsterer's tape over the top. Now open the fabric so the pattern faces you, stretch it taut, and staple the other edges.

Fabric and wall coverings lend themselves to lots of decorative ploys. You can cover the ceiling and one wall or install a small panel over the bed as a pretend canopy. Consider covering just the eaves in an attic room, or using coverings to brighten the ceiling of a hall or stairway. To help pull down a ceiling that is too high, install molding on the walls about one foot from the top, then cover the ceiling and the wall above the molding.

MAKE YOUR CEILINGS SPECIAL WITH BEAMS

Beams suggest the solid shelter of a house with a long, stable history. If your home has beamed ceilings, by all means play up these architectural assets. If it doesn't and you wish it did, you have two choices: Add them, or pull down the existing ceiling and expose the structural members. Here's how to go about either project.

Beams are at home in both formal and informal settings, but the look you want to achieve should dictate the style of the beams. If you're after a sleek, sophisticated look, trim beams with moldings or add decorative corbels at the ends, like the ones in the photo at *near right*. For a rustic look, select beams with a hand-hewn appearance.

Next you need to decide whether to put up new beams or show off joists that support the floor above, as was done in the room shown *opposite*. If your home was built after the turn of the century, you might as well forget about exposing the joists. They are probably no more attractive than the ordinary dimension lumber used to frame houses today. Also consider that removing a ceiling removes the dead air space that reduces sound transmission from one level to another.

Adding beams
If you're thinking about adding beams, you may wonder how you're going to get big heavy timbers up to the ceiling—and keep them there. The answer is that false beams don't have to support anything. They only need to *look* massive. They should, in fact, be as light as possible.

Box beams, such as the ones at *near right,* are three-sided channels assembled with lengths of 1x6 lumber. You build the channels on the floor, attach 2x2 furring strips to the ceiling (two per beam), then nail through the sides of the channels into the furring.

Even easier to work with are lightweight urethane foam beams sold at home centers. Cut them to length with a knife and glue them to the ceiling.

Exposing beams
If you are determined to show off beams long covered with plaster or other material, prepare for a messy job. Clear all furnishings from the room and protect floors with canvas drop cloths. Wearing a hardhat, goggles, and heavy gloves, begin pulling down the ceiling with a wrecking bar. You'll probably find that the ceiling comes down fairly easily, but hauling away the debris is heavy, time-consuming labor.

Beams that have been hidden for a century or so are usually filthy. Scrub them with a strong detergent. (If you prefer a lighter tone, add bleach.) Seal with a coat of matte-finish polyurethane.

MAKE YOUR CEILINGS SPECIAL

WITH PRESSED METAL

Many people call them "tin," but pressed metal ceiling panels are actually lightweight sheets of steel stamped with modular designs. Introduced in the nineteenth century to cover deteriorated plaster, pressed metal ceilings have made a comeback and are available in original designs that range from Victorian to art deco. Painted or left in its gleaming natural state, pressed metal can cap off any room in style.

Pressed metal ceilings could be called "new antiques." The metal is new, but it is stamped with the same dies used when the material was first popular, roughly from the 1890s to the 1930s.

Patterns range from large and simple square motifs to tight, intricate designs. All repeat at uniform intervals—from 3 to 24 inches—to facilitate matching. Nipples spaced 6 inches apart around the edges of the 2x8-foot panels help you put them up squarely.

You can also select pressed-metal cornices in a variety of designs, from 2½ to 10 inches deep. Cornices can be used to trim off a plain ceiling, too, or you might prefer to edge a metal ceiling with wood molding, as in the kitchen *opposite*.

Ordering material

Check the Yellow Pages of your phone book under "ceilings" and you may find a source for pressed metal in your area. If you don't, write for catalogs to the addresses listed at right. In choosing a pattern, keep in mind that a large or ornate design looks best on a high ceiling in a big room, or you might make it the only ornate touch in an otherwise restrained scheme. But if your room has a low ceiling, or is too long or too wide for its height, choose only smaller, tighter patterns.

Order samples of several patterns before you make your final choice. Then work up a scale drawing of the ceiling on graph paper to determine how many 2x8-foot panels you'll need. If pattern repeats won't fit evenly at the edges of the ceiling (and they probably won't), leave an even border of empty space around the edges. You can order filler plate to bridge the gaps between full panels and the cornice. Buy a few extra panels to allow for mistakes, and buy 10 to 20 percent more cornice material to allow for matching and fitting at the corners or jogs in a room.

Putting up a metal ceiling

First nail 1x2 furring strips 1½ inches from the edge of the ceiling around the perimeter of the room. Then install furring strips perpendicular to the joists. Space the strips 12 inches from center to center across the ceiling's length or width. If the surface is uneven, shim the furring at low spots. (More about furring on pages 56 and 57 and 112 and 113.)

You'll find the panels light but unwieldly. The work will require two people on ladders to manage each 2x8-foot panel, or one person on a ladder nailing while the other holds up the panel with a wooden T-brace. Wear leather gloves when you handle pressed metal because the edges are almost knife-sharp.

Begin on the side of the room farthest from the door. Using 1-inch nails, attach the edge of each panel to a furring strip. Lap the next panel over the edge of the first panel,

match up nipples, and nail directly through both. You'll need crosspieces of furring where panel ends join. Pressed metal cuts easily with metal shears; an electric nail gun speeds nailing.

Trimming with cornice strips

At the edges, install a border of filler plate. Lap this with cornice strips, nailing into the furring underneath. Nail the bottom cornice edge to the wall at 1-foot intervals.

Cut miter joints for the corners. At outside corners leave some overlap in the joint and close it by tapping with a hammer and the head of a large nail. Gently tamp joints at the ceiling the same way, or use a block of scrap wood instead of the nail.

Paint the ceiling with an oil-base primer and oil-base paint, or coat bare metal with clear polyurethane for a natural metal look.

Manufacturers' addresses
AA-Abbington Ceiling Co.
2149 Utica Avenue, Dept. BHG
Brooklyn, NY 11234
American Luminous Ceilings
3291 East 65th Street
Cleveland, OH 44127
Barney Brainum-Shanker Steel
70-32 83rd Street
Glendale, NY 11227
Chelsea Decorative Metal
6115 Cheena
Houston, TX 77096
W.F. Norman Corporation
P.O. Box 323
214-32 N. Cedar Street
Nevada, MO 64772

Adding a skylight costs about the same as adding a window of the same size. But with a skylight you give up nothing in privacy or wall space. Because the sun shines on a skylight more directly for more hours per day, you gain more natural light than an ordinary window can deliver. Of course, solar light is also solar heat, but skylights have one big drawback as solar heaters: When the sun goes down, they lose more heat than windows do. Here's how to decide whether adding a skylight would brighten your life without pushing your energy costs through the roof.

W here's the best place for a skylight? The answer demands that you strike a balance between interior needs and the situation outside.

Inside, just about any room within reach of the roof is a possible candidate, but some make more sense than others. Family rooms and other main living areas are naturals, as are baths and dim hallways. Bedrooms, on the other hand, aren't usually occupied during daytime, when skylighting works its main magic.

Attic spaces take on new life with a skylight or two, as you can see in the family room shown *above*. Here, fixed panes of glass set between rafters flood the sitting area with light, and back it up with a treetop view.

But before you climb up and poke a hole in your roof, consider the direction it faces. Artists may favor the quality of north light, but a north-facing roof slope is just about the worst place for a skylight. Chilly winds from that direction greatly increase heat losses.

Southern exposures pose the opposite problem in summer, when you want to minimize heat gains. Deciduous trees can help by filtering strong sunlight during the warm months. East- and west-facing slopes are about equal. Again, consider the shade value of any trees nearby.

Conserving energy

Because heat rises, a poorly insulated skylight turns into a thermal chimney that siphons off energy at night or on cool,

cloudy days when you need it most. This is why you shouldn't consider anything less than a double-glazed unit, and triple glazing is better in a cold climate.

Like any window, a skylight benefits from an insulated shade or panel that you can close at night. If access is a problem, consider rigging up cords and pulleys so you can operate the covering from below. An old-fashioned window pole also may work.

Installing a skylight

Prefabricated skylights come in a variety of sizes, typically designed to span two or three rafters on 24-inch spacings. One approach is demonstrated by the rooftop installation shown *opposite*. Rafters were left in place but beefed up for extra strength. You could choose to cut and tie off intermediate rafters for a more open look.

Skylights aren't especially difficult to install and most manufacturers provide complete instructions. However, before you decide to take on a skylight project yourself, consider these points:
• Do heights make you uncomfortable? You'll need to spend several hours on the roof, and that work should be done in one day.
• Are you knowledgeable about basic roofing and flashing techniques? Improperly installed skylights leak water and energy.
• How will light get from the roof to the room you want to brighten? If you have a flat ceiling with an attic above, you'll have to construct a light shaft through the attic, which adds to your carpentry chores.

MAKE YOUR CEILINGS SPECIAL

WITH TRACK LIGHTING

Have you ever wondered what makes a *Better Homes and Gardens*® photograph so appealing? One reason is light, beamed to emphasize some elements and put others in delicate shadow. The right lighting can help create similar effects at your house, and if you put your lighting on tracks, you can change it whenever you like.

The tracks consist of lightweight metal channels in lengths of 2, 4, and 8 feet. They plug together end-to-end or in X, L, or T layouts. You mount the tracks on the ceiling, wire them into an electrical box, then snap on fixtures wherever you need them. For more versatility, purchase tracks with two, three, or four circuits that enable you to control several sets of lights independently of each other.

Putting up tracks
Like trains, track lights can't go where there are no tracks, so plan your runs carefully. One rule of thumb suggests that you position tracks about 30 inches away from any 8-foot-high wall you want to illuminate. If your ceilings are higher, increase this distance proportionally. Better yet, experiment with clamp lights mounted to a broomstick until you achieve an effect that pleases you.

Tracks don't need to be limited to ceiling installations. If you mount one on the wall at the head of your bed, for example, you can read while your spouse sleeps.

Because they weigh only a few pounds, tracks attach to a wall or ceiling with any of the standard fasteners shown on pages 130 and 131. Wiring tracks to an electrical box is no more complicated than hooking up an ordinary light fixture. But if you don't have power in the right place, you may need to hire an electrician to install a new outlet and possibly a wall switch or switches. As an alternative, you can run heavy-duty lamp cord from the track, across the ceiling, and down the wall to a receptacle.

Selecting fixtures
Specialized spotlight and track fixtures serve just about any lighting need. The box at *right* shows just five among the 20 or more units you can choose. By fitting them with bulbs that provide different beam widths, you can create hundreds of lighting effects.

Although contemporary in appearance, the fixtures are available in off-white tones that blend with a ceiling, in solid accent colors, or in gleaming chrome finishes that call attention to themselves. In the room shown *opposite,* for example, a line of track lights plays up a dramatically sloping ceiling by day and washes the wall with soft light during evening hours.

SPOTLIGHTS

When you first set up a track installation, avoid the inclination to buy too much. You may not need as many fixtures as you think. Some fixtures (such as the *focusing spot and pin spot* shown *below*) are also available as permanent-mount canopy units.

Canister lights are most basic and least expensive. They accept both wide-beam floodlights and narrow-beam spotlights. Start by placing one every 3 or 4 feet.

With a weighted base you can turn a canister into an *uplight* that sits on the floor and dramatizes plants, artwork, or a dim corner. An adapter lets you plug into a wall receptacle.

A *focusing spot* has an adjustable beam that can be shaped precisely. It is similar to a *framing projector* (not shown), which offers greater control but is more costly.

A *pin spot* beams intense light on a small object. This one, which can be fitted with an optional colored filter, steps down power to 12 volts to save electricity.

Although they are not track fixtures, *clamp-on lamps* have the same look and versatility. Use them where you need only one or two accent lights.

MAKE YOUR CEILINGS SPECIAL

WITH HANGING GARDENS

Hanging plants lend light-and-shadow serenity to a room and conserve floor space. In situations where privacy isn't critical, they can serve as a window treatment. To make a success of a ceiling garden, you need to choose trailing species that grow well in the light available to them. Here are some pointers on how to get your ceiling green and growing.

PLANTS FOR HANGING GARDENS

	CHARACTERISTICS	COMMENTS
FOR THE SUN		
Coleus	Does well in sunlight.	Plants in this group thrive in strong sunlight and protect shade-loving plants placed behind them. Striped-leaved plants, having less chlorophyll, require more sun than dark-leaved varietals of the same species.
Sweet Potato Vine	Root one of eyes cut from tuber to grow vine.	
Rattail Cactus	Has trailing stems; especially suited for hanging.	
Ivy-Leaved Geranium	Leaves like ivy; flowers on trailing stems.	
String of Beads	An African succulent; creeping stems, white florets.	
Glory Pea	From Australia, with silver leaves and red flowers.	
Star-of-Bethlehem	Fragile, but produces masses of blue or white flowers.	
Black-Eyed Susan	Flourishes in baskets as well as pots.	

	CHARACTERISTICS	COMMENTS
FOR THE SHADE		
Wax Plant	Grow well in partial shade.	Trailers that spread down are especially desirable. Try foliage plants from shady forest floors: Maidenhair Fern, Boston Fern, Basket Grass, Red Ivy, English Ivy, Swedish Ivy, Wandering Jew.
Goldfish Vine		
Hot Water Plant		
Fuchsia (trailing)		
Staghorn Fern	A showy specimen worth trying here.	
Philodendron	Always works, but get some of more unusual varieties.	
Spider Plant	Trailing offshoots, invites starting whole collection from parent plant.	
Baby's-tears	Delicate in scale, but adds grace note with tendrils spilling over pot's edge.	

A hanging garden might consist of one showy plant such as a fern, or it might be a lush combination of species. Whether plants do well depends mainly on the light available.

Check exposure to sunlight at several times during a clear day. (If you're a photographer, use a light meter.) When is the light strong enough to cast a shadow, and for how long? What is likely to happen in other seasons? Consider points in the room several feet below the ceiling, not at floor level.

As a rule, windows facing south get the strongest light, while north-facing windows receive weak but steady light. East windows enjoy cool morning light, but west light can be hot, especially on summer afternoons.

Many rooms have two or more exposures. However, if natural light isn't adequate, supplement it with artificial light. Ultraviolet plant lights work best, but ordinary incandescent and fluorescent bulbs also emit most of the rays a plant needs.

Hanging your plants
A large plant in a pot of water-logged earth can weigh as much as 30 pounds, so provide secure moorings (see pages 130 and 131). In some cases you may want to install expansion- or toggle-bolt hooks in the ceiling. In other cases a bracket attached to a wall or window frame might be a better approach.

Consider how you will water your hanging plants. Will you need a stepladder? Unusually high plants can be raised and lowered with a pulley.

For ultimate flexibility, consider rolling your plants along a track, like the one in the sun-room *opposite*. This arrangement lets you adjust groupings or shift plants to follow the sun from season to season. (More about this track and other plant-hanging ideas on pages 120 and 121.)

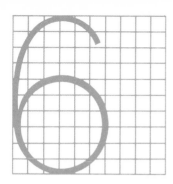

PLANNING WALL AND CEILING CHANGES

A successful improvement project, like a successful journey, begins with a clear picture of where you're going. Just as you would be wise to consult a map before you set off on a trip, so should you draw up a plan of attack before beginning any but the simplest of projects. If you try your ideas on paper first, you might be spared the trouble and expense of changes later. This chapter shows how to measure and diagram your rooms, how to sketch wall and ceiling changes you may be thinking about, and how to develop a scale plan that you or a contractor can follow. Then all you need to do is work up a materials list and decide who will do the work.

GETTING STARTED

What will happen to a room if you add much-needed storage? Could you still fit in the furnishings you have? Should you build one big closet or two smaller ones? Before you can answer questions such as these, you need to know exactly what you're starting with. This means drawing a "before" plan of the room as it is.

Begin with a freehand sketch of the room or rooms you're thinking about. Don't worry at this point about precise proportions and absolutely straight lines. What you're aiming for is a rough drawing, like the plan shown *opposite*, on which you can note measurements. Start by drawing a square or rectangle, whatever shape the room happens to be, then indicate the locations of doors, windows, air registers, electrical outlets and other elements that are fixed parts of the room. The best way to do this is to stand in the center of the room and draw each wall in order as you turn to face it. Keep going until you're facing the wall you started with. Then go around once more to make sure you didn't leave out any elements.

Next, start measuring. A retractable metal tape works best (you may need a helper to hold one end). Don't attempt simply to pace off distances or flip-flop a yardstick along the wall. Measure the width of door and window openings, and the distances between openings. Note which way doors swing, and where wall switches, electrical receptacles, and heating/cooling registers are located. (To learn the customary symbols for these items, see pages 98 and 152-155.)

As you take each measurement, indicate it on your sketch with lines and arrows, as was done on the sample. To make sure you leave nothing out, take all measurements in sequence as you move around the room. When you reach the point where you started, take your sketch to the center of the room and slowly turn around again, checking to make sure you haven't left anything out. Check the accuracy of your measurements by totaling the individual dimensions along each wall to see whether they add up to the wall's overall length.

Making elevation drawings
After you complete the rough floor plan, you may decide you also want a rough *elevation* drawing of one or more of the walls. Elevations map out dimensions on vertical surfaces, information you'll need to know before you can plan changes that affect walls. After you sketch a rough elevation, measure the height of doors and windows, the distance from windowsills to the floor, and any other vertical dimensions that affect the project.

With both plan and elevation drawings, you can't be *too* careful about measurements. If you make a mistake at this stage, it will almost certainly come back to haunt you. But if you catch errors now, all it takes is an eraser and a pencil to correct them.

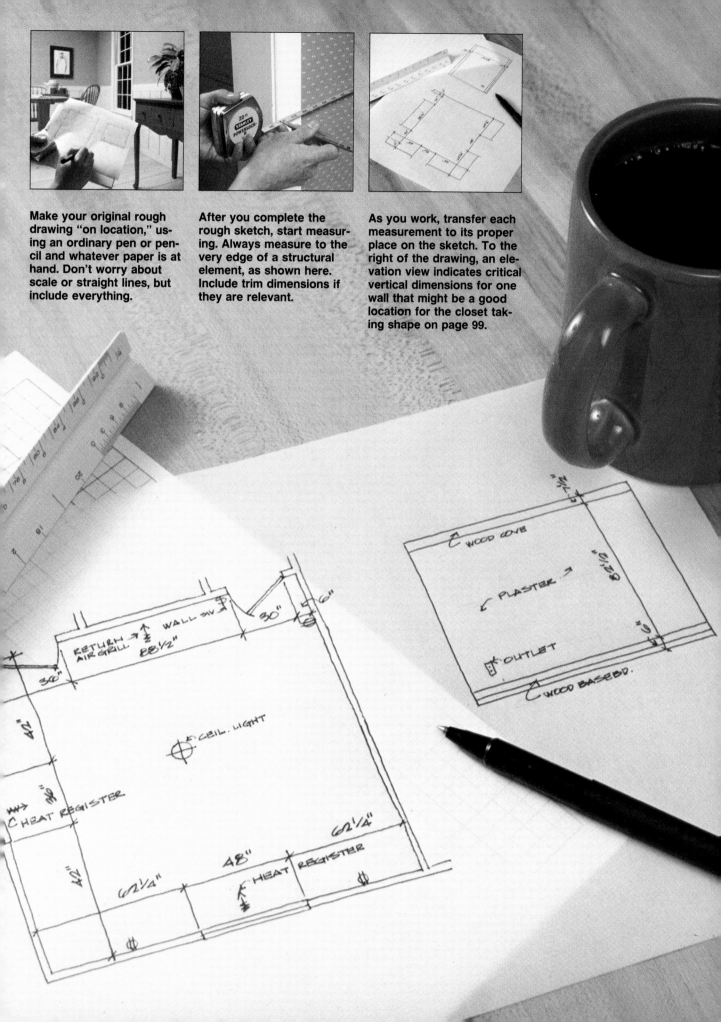

Make your original rough drawing "on location," using an ordinary pen or pencil and whatever paper is at hand. Don't worry about scale or straight lines, but include everything.

After you complete the rough sketch, start measuring. Always measure to the very edge of a structural element, as shown here. Include trim dimensions if they are relevant.

As you work, transfer each measurement to its proper place on the sketch. To the right of the drawing, an elevation view indicates critical vertical dimensions for one wall that might be a good location for the closet taking shape on page 99.

DRAWING TO SCALE

Now that you know all your room's vital statistics, it's time to convert your rough sketch into a precisely scaled *mechanical*. A mechanical drawing is one made with instruments.

The "instruments" you'll need appear in the photos on this page: a sharp pencil or pen, graph paper, tracing paper, masking tape, a clear plastic triangle, and an architect's scale. A typical architect's scale actually includes six scales, two on each of its three sides. Select the largest scale that will allow you to fit your room onto the paper. Usually a scale of ½ inch to the foot works well. If that scale works for you, buy graph paper with ½-inch squares.

Tape a piece of tracing paper over the graph paper and begin to draw your room. To render an 8-foot-long wall, draw a line eight squares long. Use the architect's scale to check your graph-paper counts and to draw fractional lengths.

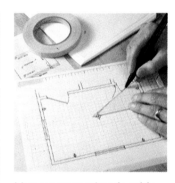

Line up your triangle with squares on graph paper to help draw straight lines. Curves can be made freehand. The box, below left, shows common symbols.

FLOOR PLAN SYMBOLS

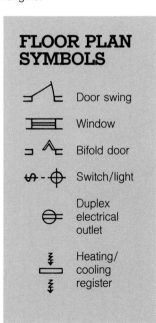

Door swing

Window

Bifold door

Switch/light

Duplex electrical outlet

Heating/ cooling register

PLANNING WITH
TRACING PAPER

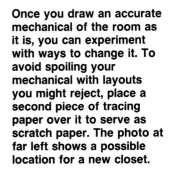

Once you draw an accurate mechanical of the room as it is, you can experiment with ways to change it. To avoid spoiling your mechanical with layouts you might reject, place a second piece of tracing paper over it to serve as scratch paper. The photo at far left shows a possible location for a new closet.

Perhaps two closets, one on each side of a window, would be better. It takes only a few minutes to get a clear picture, as shown in the near left photo.

The final test of a floor plan is whether your furnishings will fit into the changed space. To find out, make scaled cutouts or templates of major pieces and move them into your "new" room. In the photo at left cutouts represent a game table, sofa, coffee table, and desk with chair.

OTHER DRAWINGS YOU MAY NEED

Remember the rough elevation drawing shown on page 97? Your planning project may require a finished, mechanical elevation view as well. An elevation shows how a wall appears when you view it straight on. You don't need one if there's nothing out of the ordinary about the wall you plan to change. Door openings, electrical receptacles, and other standard features can be indicated on the floor plan. If you hand a carpenter a floor plan with no elevations or other views, you'll get a plain, featureless wall or walls.

On the other hand, if there's something special you want to tell about a wall—a molding treatment, for example, or a built-in unit—use tracing paper, graph paper, and your other drafting tools to show how it would look if your line of sight were exactly perpendicular to the plane of the wall.

The photos at *right* show an elevation of our proposed closet taking shape. Check the version *above* to see how two sets of bifold doors span a 60-inch-wide opening. Also note that the lower section of the wall to the left of the opening is to include wainscoting.

The finished elevation *below* tells even more about the way we want the doors to look, and it includes notes about trim and other features. With any elevation drawing, be as specific and detailed as possible, even if you are the only one who will use it. Why? Because an accurate elevation drawing clearly portrays what you have in mind. If you don't like what you see, get out another piece of tracing paper and try again. Second, an elevation gives precise dimensions you can use to make a list of the materials you'll need for a project.

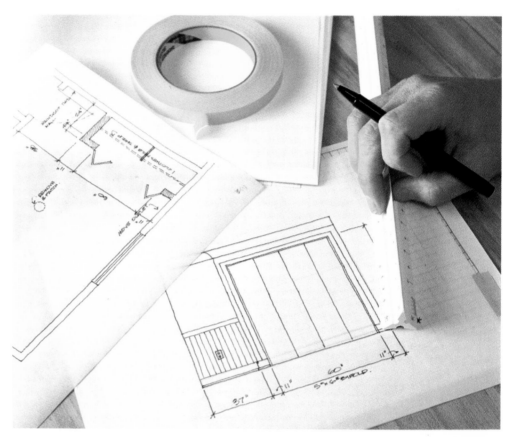

BASIC PLANNING DIMENSIONS

Passage doors:
2'6" wide x 6'8" high

Passage openings
(no door):
2'8" wide x 6'8" high

Hallways: 36" wide

Closets: 24" deep

Electrical switch from
floor: 40½" to center

Electrical receptacle
from floor: 11½" to
center

Wainscot height from
floor: 36"

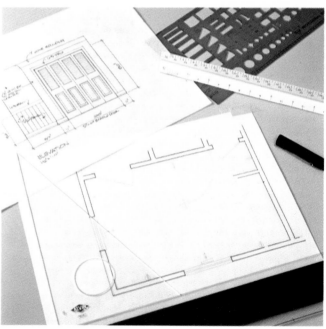

WHAT TO GIVE THE WORKMAN

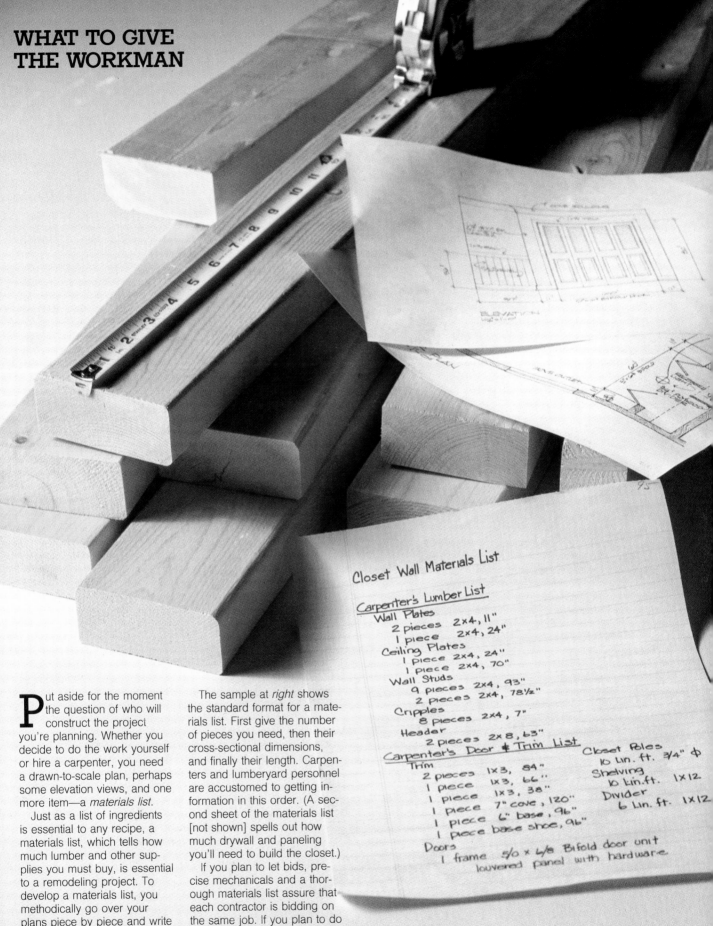

Closet Wall Materials List

Carpenter's Lumber List

Wall Plates
   2 pieces   2x4, 11"
   1 piece   2x4, 24"

Ceiling Plates
   1 piece 2x4, 24"
   1 piece 2x4, 70"

Wall Studs
   9 pieces 2x4, 93"
   2 pieces 2x4, 78½"

Cripples
   8 pieces 2x4, 7"

Header
   2 pieces 2x8, 63"

Carpenter's Door & Trim List

Trim
   2 pieces 1x3, 84"
   1 piece   1x3, 66"
   1 piece   1x3, 38"
   1 piece   7" cove, 120"
   1 piece   6" base, 96"
   1 piece base shoe, 96"

Doors
   1 frame 5/0 x 6/8 Bifold door unit
      louvered panel with hardware

Closet Poles
   10 Lin. ft. ¾" ⌀
Shelving
   10 Lin. ft. 1x12
Divider
   6 Lin. ft. 1x12

Put aside for the moment the question of who will construct the project you're planning. Whether you decide to do the work yourself or hire a carpenter, you need a drawn-to-scale plan, perhaps some elevation views, and one more item—a *materials list*.

Just as a list of ingredients is essential to any recipe, a materials list, which tells how much lumber and other supplies you must buy, is essential to a remodeling project. To develop a materials list, you methodically go over your plans piece by piece and write down every single item.

The sample at *right* shows the standard format for a materials list. First give the number of pieces you need, then their cross-sectional dimensions, and finally their length. Carpenters and lumberyard personnel are accustomed to getting information in this order. (A second sheet of the materials list [not shown] spells out how much drywall and paneling you'll need to build the closet.)

If you plan to let bids, precise mechanicals and a thorough materials list assure that each contractor is bidding on the same job. If you plan to do the work, you can proceed with confidence, knowing that you have fully rehearsed the project on paper.

PLANNING WALL AND CEILING CHANGES

WHEN DOES IT PAY TO DO WORK YOURSELF?

Have you ever wondered whether you really save money by doing around-the-house chores yourself? After all, if you're a wage-earner, your time is worth money, too. Mightn't you be better off to hire a professional and perhaps take on a "moon-lighting" project or two to pay for the work? The answer, from a strictly financial point of view, is *almost never*.

One big reason is that labor costs for household jobs routinely run $10 to $15 an hour, and have risen to more than $20 an hour in some parts of the country.

What's more, you also must reckon with the fact that you would be paying for most of the work in after-tax earnings. Consider, for example, that work on your house requires a carpenter who will cost $10 an hour, or $80 a day, a modest rate by today's standards. If you are in the 28 percent tax bracket, to offset the carpenter's $10-an-hour rate, you must earn $14 an hour before taxes ($112 a day). If you were to pay a $16-an-hour carpenter for a job—not an uncommon rate today—your extra income before taxes must be more than $22 an hour to offset the bill. Doing the job yourself could save a considerable amount of money. If you're able, you might find it to your advantage to take off a few days or a week from your job at no pay to do essential high-cost work on your house. However, as with many other matters, economics isn't the only consideration. Here are other factors you need to take into account.

Can you do it yourself?
To gain any significant savings by doing the job yourself, you must be reasonably proficient with tools and have the time and patience to do the job well. Realistically gauge your own capability and stamina for doing the work.

But don't be intimidated by a project because you've never done it before. Many home improvement jobs are much less mystifying than you might think, thanks to new products designed for trouble-free installation. Stroll through a home center and you'll find dozens of items packaged expressly for do-it-yourselfers.

This doesn't mean that an unskilled amateur can successfully tackle any or all work on a house. Unless you've got the aptitude, plus the willingness to learn how to do new work, leave difficult jobs to professionals. In other words, know your own limitations and act accordingly. Refer to the chart *opposite* for help in assessing the difficulty of common wall and ceiling projects.

How long will it take?
Your free time may be worth more than dollars to you. Consider that it usually will take an amateur more hours than a pro to complete a job. The longer it takes you, the less you save.

Any job that can be completed in a weekend or two is a good candidate for a do-it-yourselfer. If you undertake a big job in a high-traffic area of your home, you and the rest of the family must be prepared to live with the mess. Also consider whether the job will disrupt plumbing and electricity, and for how long. Conversion of an out-of-the-way attic may be a better choice than retiling a heavily used bathroom.

Where are your greatest savings?
You'll save the most money when you tackle a job for which labor takes the biggest share of the total cost.

Most common home-improvement jobs break down roughly to a 50-50 split between the cost of labor and materials. There are exceptions, of course, including remodeling a kitchen or bathroom. In these projects, more of the cost goes for the materials (new cabinets, fixtures, appliances) than for the labor to install them. On the other hand, labor can account for a much larger share of many wall and ceiling projects, as the chart explains.

If you're in doubt about the labor quotient of a particular job, and thus whether you'll save much by doing it yourself, talk with a few contractors. What hourly rate do they charge? How does it compare with the cost of the entire job?

Dividing up the work
Many wall and ceiling jobs lend themselves nicely to a division of labor. That means you hire a contractor to do some of the work; you do the rest. You don't save as much, but you significantly reduce the risk of a botched or sloppy-looking job. Consider this alternative if any part of the project appears to be beyond the level of your handyman skills. The jobs that the average home-owner can do without undue risk of failure are usually those that fall at the beginning of a project: tearing out walls, taking out fixtures and appliances, removing wallpaper and paint. These are all dirty, disagreeable tasks, but almost anyone can do them. If you need to save money, do these jobs yourself instead of paying a skilled workman, or consider hiring a less skilled laborer to work with you. At the other end of the job, you can put up tile, install fixtures, paint, and hang paper.

If you hire a contractor
The more planning you do in the initial stages, the less likely you are to be unpleasantly surprised at billing time. Even if you're not going to do the work yourself, have a good idea of what the job entails. This will ensure that you don't end up with less than you paid for or more than you wanted. Get separate quotes on the material and labor charges. It may pay for you to buy and haul the materials yourself, rather than pay for the time of a skilled workman to do this portion of the job. If possible, keep track of how the job progresses. Not only will you be able to keep your eye on the workman, but you'll also be able to deal with unforeseen problems while things are still in the construction stage.

The intangibles
Doing it yourself has its own special rewards and satisfactions. Often you'll do a better job yourself, if only because outside workers, however skilled, seldom apply the care to your home that you do.

ASSESSING WALL AND CEILING JOBS

	PROJECT	% LABOR	COMMENTS
MOST AMATEURS CAN DO	**Paint**	90	Painting is labor-intensive because lots of prep work goes into a good job. Pages 146-149 tell how to repair surfaces; pages 40-43, how to paint them.
	Wall covering	75	Some types are tricky to work with, but most coverings are only a little more difficult to put up than a new coat of paint. Pages 44-47 tell how.
	Paneling	60	Some do-it-yourselfers find paneling easier to work with than wallpaper, or even paint. If you can accurately measure and cut straight lines, there's no reason you shouldn't consider taking on a paneling job yourself. To learn what's involved, see pages 54-61.
REQUIRE MODERATE DO-IT-YOURSELF SKILLS	**Ceramic tile**	60	Tiling a wall calls for patience, mastery of a few basic techniques, and a few specialized tools, most of which you can rent from a tile dealer. Pages 70 and 71 take you through a tiling job.
	Acoustic tile and suspended ceilings	50	Here materials and installation techniques have been designed with amateurs in mind. Pages 112 and 113 show how to put up acoustic tile; pages 114 and 115 tell about suspended ceilings.
	Drywall	60	Drywall panels cut easily and go up fast, but taping and smoothing the joints between them is a job many amateurs find tricky and tedious. Pages 108-111 picture all the steps involved in a typical drywalling project.
	Insulating	70	Whether or not insulating is a feasible do-it-yourself project depends largely upon what you're insulating. Unfinished attics are easy, finished walls next to impossible. Pages 136-140 tell about insulating basics.
HIRE A PROFESSIONAL	**Removing bearing walls**		Percentages are meaningless here because any task that will alter your home's support systems or expose its interior to weather should be delegated to skilled professionals.
	Extensive changes to exterior walls		

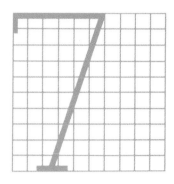

HOW TO BUILD NEW WALLS AND CEILINGS

If you can make accurate cuts with a handsaw and can hit a nail squarely on the head, you can create new walls and ceilings. The materials you'll need are inexpensive and, for the most part, easy to work with. Few home improvements can add so much new living space in so little time. In this chapter, you'll learn the basics of framing and finishing partition walls, the easy ways to put up a new ceiling, and the most up-to-date way to insulate a cathedral ceiling.

FRAMING A PARTITION

Framing a partition that doesn't have to support the ceiling isn't difficult, but it does require careful planning and good work habits. Go slowly at first, and double-check all measurements before you begin. When planning cuts, remember that your basic material, the common 2x4, actually measures only 1½x3½ inches.

Although most partitions are framed with wood, you can also use metal studs. They have the same dimensions as their wood cousins and are lightweight and easy to work with. A dealer can tell if you would save money by working with metal.

Measure for measure
The first step is to figure the dimensions of the partitions you plan to build. Although the standard ceiling height is 8 feet, the ceiling height may be different in your house. Older homes often have higher ceilings, and basements often have lower ones. If the floor is carpeted, remove the carpeting (or slit it and fold it back) from the places where the new partitions will stand. Measure the distance from the floor to the bottom of the ceiling or ceiling joists. Do this in several places along the line of the partitions to see whether there is any unevenness to take into account.

As you start making measurements, sketch out the framework of the partitions on graph paper. Individual studs, which are vertical framing members spaced at intervals within a wall, should be located 16 inches apart (measured from the centers of adjoining studs). If you're going to install a door, try to have one side of

the opening fall at a regular stud location. This will save you a little on material costs.

Picking the pieces
With sketch in hand, go to your lumber dealer and ask for help selecting materials. Buy "stud-grade" lumber that is free of loose knots or major warpage. Be especially choosy about the quality of the pieces you'll be using for bottom and top plates, those parts of the wall running perpendicularly to the studs. If you plan to hang a door, you'll also need material for a *header*, which is heavier framing in a wall (usually doubled and laid on edge) at the top of a door or other opening. The instructions that come with the door should indicate the dimensions of the header and the size of the rough opening to leave in the partition.

If price is no object, consider buying precut studs. They're less than 8 feet long and are cut to fit between the top and bottom plates in a standard 8-foot-high space. A dealer can help determine whether you will be able to use precut studs.

You'll also need plenty of 16-penny nails and, if you'll be working on a cement floor, some masonry fasteners. Again, trust a dealer to help you decide on the best materials and tools for the job.

On the next three pages are descriptions of ways to make a partition: prefabbing it on the floor, framing it in place, and framing it with metal.

(continued)

PREFRAMING ON THE FLOOR

1 Cut three 2x4s to length for top, bottom, and sole plates. (A sole plate is the bottommost horizontal part of a stud partition.) Place the top and bottom plates together, and lay out the location of each stud. Allow 16 inches from the center of one stud to the center of the next. At the door locations, follow instructions supplied with the door.

4 At doors, frame an opening that meets your door manufacturer's requirements. Fasten the header between studs, then support the header with trimmer studs on each side. Don't cut out the bottom plate until you are ready to install the door. Make certain the finished opening matches the rough opening dimensions for the door.

2 Snap a chalk line to mark the location of the outside edge of the sole plate. Make sure the line is at a right angle to adjoining walls. Nail the sole plate to the floor. Use masonry nails or a power nailer if the floor is masonry (see photo). You can rent a power nailer. To smooth out minor unevenness, wedge tapered shims between the floor and the plate.

5 Raise the wall into place on top of the sole plate and brace it temporarily. Shim any minor irregularities between the sole and bottom plates with thin strips of wood, as shown. If your new wall will run perpendicular to ceiling joists or be directly under them, you can nail its top plate directly to the joists. If not, you'll need to install a 2x6 nailer up there as shown in photo number 6.

3 Cut studs to length, taking into account the 4½-inch thickness of the three plates. Lay out the studs on the floor between the top and bottom plates. If the studs are bowed, arrange them so they all bow in the same direction. Nail the wall together, driving two 16-penny nails through the top plate and two through the bottom plate.

6 If you need a nailer, nail supports between joists at 16-inch intervals and attach the nailer to them. It should be even with the joists' bottom edges. Be sure the wall is where you want it, then nail through the top plate into the joists or ceiling nailer and through the bottom plate into the sole plate.

TOENAILING

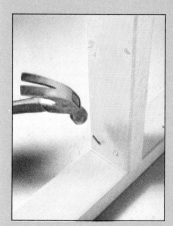

1 Cut studs for a snug fit between the top and bottom plates. Start a nail into the stud at about a 45-degree angle. Drive the nail until it just begins to break through the bottom face of the stud. Use two on one side of the stud and one centered on the other side. Position the stud slightly away from the location line. As you drive the nails, the stud should slide into place.

2 After you drive the first nail, make sure the stud is in the proper position and isn't twisted. If everything is right, drive the other two nails into the stud and plate. Before nailing the stud into the top plate, make sure it will be perfectly plumb. Drive in the nails so their heads fit securely against the inside face of the stud.

3 To make the job easier at first, cut a nailing spacer from a scrap of 2x4. For studs that are spaced 16 inches apart on center, make the spacer 14½ inches long. Move the spacer from stud to stud as you proceed along the wall. As an alternative to using a spacer, enlist a helper to hold a heavy hammer or mallet against the opposite side of the stud.

Assembling a stud wall on the floor makes sense for a relatively short wall on a relatively level floor. With longer runs and on uneven terrain, many carpenters prefer to install plates top and bottom, custom-cut studs to fit between them, and nail the studs into their final, vertical positions. If you decide to work this way, you'll have to learn one of the most basic skills in carpentry: toenailing. Toenailing means driving nails at an angle, usually through a stud and into a plate.

The trick to performing this job well is preventing the stud from moving out of place as you drive the nails. If possible, you should practice on scrap wood or make a spacing aid before attempting to toenail a stud in place. The box at *left* shows how to achieve high-quality work.

Metal studs

If you want to avoid toenailing, use metal studs. Although used for years in commercial work, metal studs are relatively unknown among do-it-yourselfers. That's too bad because metal studs offer several advantages over wood. They won't warp in damp places, and each stud is perfectly straight and uniform.

Because the studs are joined with self-tapping, sheet-metal screws, you might want to buy a power screwdriver to speed the work. Bear in mind that a metal-framed wall is surprisingly fragile until covered with drywall. Use caution when working with metal studs so you don't accidentally damage them. Metal studs have little compressive strength, so don't use them for load-bearing walls or walls supporting heavy shelves.

Metal studs are usually galvanized steel, and they come in a variety of sizes and shapes. The most common types are the C stud and the channel stud. The C stud has a cross section resembling a squared-off C. The channel stud (pictured in the photograph *opposite*) is shaped like a U. In place of plates, metal studs fit into tracks at the top and bottom of a wall.

The webbing (the wide face) of metal studs may be solid or prepunched with holes for conduit and pipes. You can buy studs in a number of different dimensions, but for simplicity's sake, you'll probably want to purchase those measuring 1½x3½ inches—the same size as a nominal 2x4 stud.

If you use metal studs, follow the door manufacturer's instructions when framing doors and other openings. Your dealer may be able to cut the plates to the needed dimensions if you don't want to do it yourself. Otherwise, plan to get a good pair of metal snips.

Handling the corners

Turning a corner with studs requires assembling a corner post. The box *opposite, below* shows the two most common types. Don't try to save materials here. Corner posts are important because they provide stability where two walls meet. They also provide nailing surfaces for wall finishes.

FRAMING WITH METAL

1 Metal studs are so light that you don't have to build walls on the floor first. Just screw top and bottom tracks to the ceiling and floor. Use a plumb bob or a string and weight to make certain the two tracks are directly under each other. Cut both studs and tracks with tin snips.

2 After the tracks are secured, slip each stud into them sideways. Move each stud into position and give it a twist at top and bottom. You'll feel a firm snap as it locks into place in the track. Continue moving down the wall until all studs are in their proper positions.

3 Check all studs for plumb. Make sure any rough openings for doors are properly sized and squared. To lock studs into place, use special self-tapping, sheet-metal screws. If you have a lot of fastening to do, buy or rent a power screwdriver or use a screwdriver bit in an electric drill.

4 Attach gypsum drywall to the studs with screws, driving the screws until their heads are just below the surface of the drywall. The framing won't be sturdy until the drywall is securely fastened to it.

TURNING A CORNER

1 Build this type of corner post from three full-length 2x4s and some short spacer pieces. Sandwich the spacers between two of the 2x4s, and nail them together. Then nail the third 2x4 at a right angle to the first two. Instead of spacers, a fourth 2x4 also will work. If you use metal studs, see photo number 2, at *right*.

2 This corner post is becoming more popular because it requires just three 2x4s. When you install corner posts, make sure there are nailing surfaces for finish materials, such as drywall, outside and inside the corner. Fasten metal studs to each other and to their tracks with self-tapping screws.

PUTTING UP DRYWALL

CUTTING

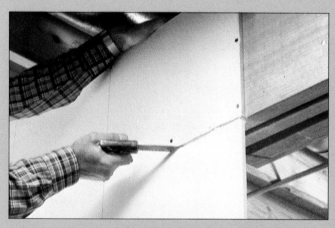

1 Cutting drywall to size is easy. To avoid too much cutting, however, arrange the panels as economically as possible.

To cut installed drywall, use a fine-tooth keyhole saw. To cut holes for electrical boxes, drill a hole in each corner to make starting easier. You also can buy drywall saws that cut down on the need for drilling holes. Holes that must be located in precise spots should be cut before you install the drywall (see photo number 5).

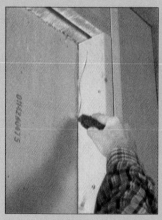

2 The simplest way to cut drywall is to score the paper facing with a razor knife, then snap the free end of the board back. The drywall should break cleanly at the score. After the core is free, slit the paper on the back of the board. It takes experience to get the knack of making clean breaks, so practice on scraps until you develop a feel for how to do it.

3 Make door cutouts using a saw or by scoring and bending the board. When cutting into drywall, always inspect the edges of the panel. If they're particularly rough or ragged, smooth them with a file or rasp. If the edges of the cut won't show—at an outlet or switch, for example—don't bother to smooth them.

4 When working around pipes and electrical boxes, you need to measure carefully. Measure the location of the opening just before you install the panel. Take your measurements from the floor or ceiling and from the edge of the adjacent installed panel. Transfer the measurements to the new panel and make your cuts before installing it.

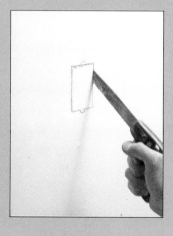

5 Make the cutouts for pipes and electrical boxes a little larger than the dimensions of the pipe or box. Cover plates will hide the exposed edges. Cut slots from the edges of the panel if you can't disassemble pipes or other projections. In some cases, you may have to put together smaller pieces of drywall to accommodate a fixture. If so, be sure the edges of the panel are supported.

Until the 1950s, plastering was the most popular way to finish residential walls. A versatile relative of cement, plaster is ideal for covering odd shapes or curves, and can be applied in a variety of textures and finishes. Nevertheless, working with plaster requires a lot of time and skill—two things amateur wall-builders often don't have.

Drywall, also known as gypsum board, wallboard, or Sheetrock (a trade name), is almost as versatile as plaster and can be applied by most do-it-yourselfers. To achieve professional results, however, you still have to invest a fair amount of time and effort.

Plaster sandwich
Drywall is a sandwich of brittle gypsum plaster between outer layers of tough paper. Like other building materials, it comes in many types, each suited to a particular purpose. For the most part, you'll be using one of three kinds.
• *Regular drywall* is produced in panels that are 4 feet wide and 6, 8, 10, or 12 feet long. The long edges are tapered so that joints can be covered with a paper tape and filled with a special compound to produce a smooth finish. The most common thickness is ½ inch, although ⅝-inch-thick drywall also is popular. Use regular drywall for most partitions.
• *Water-resistant drywall.* In wet areas around the house—bathrooms and kitchens, for example—select drywall that resists water damage. This material most often is used as a base for ceramic tiles, and comes in ½- and ⅝-inch thicknesses. It's typically light blue or green, in contrast to regular panels, which are gray.

• *Type X drywall* has additives in its core that make it more fire-resistant. Most local building codes specify just where Type X drywall must be used. Walls between garages and living spaces are a common example.

Specialized forms of drywall abound. Some have distinctive finishes, and others help to cut the transmission of noise through the wall. You also can buy foil-backed drywall. The foil acts as a vapor barrier and reflects heat back into living spaces. Ask a drywall dealer for details on special products.

Be gentle, yet tough
Although drywall is a handy building material, it does have a couple of character defects. First, the material is easily damaged until it is installed. Edges are especially vulnerable, so stack the sheets on their faces.

The other problem is more substantial: Drywall is heavy. A 4x8-foot sheet of ½-inch drywall weighs about 65 pounds. With walls, you can tilt panels into place, as shown at *right*, but you should have help when working on ceilings. If possible, rent a lift used for installing ceiling panels.

How you fasten drywall in place is a matter of choice. Nails, screws, or adhesive will do. For each option, however, there are products designed specifically for use with drywall. Be sure the fasteners you choose are the right type.
(continued)

FASTENING

1 Before installing drywall, mark the position of studs on the face of the panel. Adjoining panels should meet at the center of a stud. Never apply drywall with an unsupported edge. Add an extra stud if necessary. Test-fit the panel before attaching it firmly to the wall studs.

2 Carefully put the panel in place; tack the upper corners first, or have a helper hold the panel. If you use adhesive, carefully follow the manufacturer's directions. If you use nails or screws, be sure you have the proper type for the drywall you plan to install. Above all, make sure that edges are perpendicular to the floor and ceiling.

3 If you use nails or screws, drive pairs into each stud at 12-inch intervals. Hammer nails until the heads are flush with the surface of the paper. Then give the nail one last blow to set the head slightly below the surface of the facing. Don't break the paper; only a slight dimple is necessary. Drive screws until the heads are just below the surface.

PUTTING UP DRYWALL

(continued)

O nce your drywall is in place, consider taking a day off. After muscling panels around, you'll need to catch your breath and calm down a bit because the next step, finishing the joints, is a delicate task.

Finishing touches

Obtaining glass-smooth joints with drywall is the mark of a professional. The process seems simple when you read about it, and, in fact, learning to finish joints isn't unusually difficult. But you have to go slowly at first. Only time can give you a feeling for just the right touch.

Start working in the least conspicuous area of the room. If you get hung up at some point, take a break. Overworking the joint compound by applying it and reapplying it can cause problems later.

The tools and materials needed to finish drywall joints are few and inexpensive. Premixed joint compound is the material that fills the joints and covers nailheads. (Gooey when wet, it dries to a smooth, slick finish.) Buy three gallons for each 500 square feet of drywall. You'll also need perforated drywall tape, 250 feet for every 500 square feet. The tape strengthens the joint and stabilizes the relatively thick layers of compound. For outside corners where the fragile edges of drywall are exposed, you'll need metal corner beads. These are nailed to corners and finished with compound.

The tools you'll need are 4- and 10-inch finishing knives. They look like oversize putty knives, but their broader edges help achieve smooth results.

You also might want a large mason's trowel for smoothing wide joints, and an inside corner tool, which looks like a finishing knife bent into a V-shape.

If you plan to finish ceiling-mounted drywall, you'll need a sturdy surface to stand on. A table is fine for small jobs, but you may have to move it as you tape a long joint, which can cause problems. Instead, set up two or three sawhorses (or chairs), and lay a couple of planks on them. Wear safety glasses and a dust mask when working on ceiling joints to keep dust and joint compound out of your eyes and mouth.

Take your time

The photographs and instructions on these two pages are a basic guide to finishing joints. Before beginning, budget extra time for the first stage—applying the tape. If you do this correctly, the finishing stages will proceed more smoothly.

After all the joints are completed and dry, sand them lightly, then go to a primer and a final finish. Flat interior paint is the most common finish, but you also can use special compounds to give the wall a rougher look and feel. These texture paints make less-than-perfect joints look better than they are. On the other hand, no paint job can overcome serious defects in the finish. Defects can be prevented, however, if you take a little extra time to do the job.

FINISHING DRYWALL JOIN'

1 Before starting, remove any grease marks or loose dirt from the joint areas. Using the 4-inch knife, apply a uniform coat of compound to the tapered joint area. The idea is to *almost* fill the depressed area. Nontapered end joints should receive a thin coat of joint compound. Work slowly and wipe the knife often to keep the compound from hardening on the blade.

2 Next, center joint tape over the compound. Using the edge of the knife, press the tape into the compound. As you move along the joint, the compound should ooze through the holes in the tape, then be carried along the tape by the knife. When you are done, the tape should be firmly embedded in the joint compound. Seams that aren't tapered also should be covered with tape and a thin coat of compound.

3 While the taped joints are drying, cover all exposed nailheads with compound. (The heads should be slightly recessed below the surface of the surrounding drywall.) Use the smaller knife to fill the depressions and smooth the compound.

4 The taped joints will take about 24 hours to dry. Next, apply a light second coat of compound with the 10-inch knife. Feather the edges of the joints, carrying a thin layer of compound out 2 inches on each side of the taper. At seams that aren't tapered, feather the compound out 7 to 9 inches. Don't overwork the joint, but do try for as smooth a finish as possible.

5 After the second coat has dried completely, rub the joint with a damp sponge or sand the surface very lightly. (Don't sand the paper tape's surface.) Apply a thin final coat of compound to the joint with the wide knife. Spread the edges of the final coat about 12 inches wide. The finished surface should be just slightly higher than the surrounding wall.

6 Because the exposed edges of drywall are fragile, they should be protected with metal channels at the outside corners. Corner beads can be cut to length with a hacksaw, and then applied to the corner with drywall nails. Drive the nails through the drywall and into the framing behind, spacing the nails about 5 inches apart.

7 Apply compound to the bead with the 4-inch knife, working one side of the corner at a time. The first coat can be relatively heavy. Use the small raised area at the center of the bead as a guide for the knife. After the first coat dries, apply one or two more coats of compound, feathering the edges into the adjoining drywall.

8 Handle inside corners with compound and paper tape. First, cut the tape to length, then fold it in half lengthwise. Apply the first layer of compound to each side of the joint, then press the creased tape into the corner. Embed the tape in the compound and allow the joint to dry.

9 Apply the finish coats of compound to the joint with a corner tool (shown in the photograph). Press the tool lightly into the corner so you don't accidentally break the paper tape. Feather the edges of the joint, using a 4-inch knife. Work one side of the corner, let it dry, and then do the other. After all the joints are dry, sand them lightly and apply paint or some other finish.

INSTALLING ACOUSTIC TILE

ATTACHING TILES TO FURRING

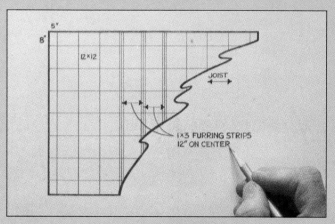

1 Acoustic tile is a quick and inexpensive way to get a good-looking ceiling where none existed before. The items you need for installation are the tiles themselves, a staple gun, 1x3-inch furring strips, thin wood shims, and scrap lumber.

Planning is the key to trouble-free installation. Sketch the ceiling, including the location of joists and obstructions such as pipes and ducts. Overlay the sketch with lines spaced at 12-inch intervals. They will indicate how many furring strips you need and where to put them. Each tile measures 12 inches square, so figuring the number to do the job is not difficult. Buy a few extra tiles in case you accidentally damage some.

2 Nail the 1x3-inch furring strips that will support the tiles so they're perpendicular to the joists. At the sidewalls, where no joist is available, build a simple backing unit for the furring. The job at *left* has 1x8s for the uprights and a 2x8 for the nailer.

3 Nail the first furring strip at the exact center of the room. Nail the remaining strips 12 inches apart from center to center. Make sure the furring strips are even. Check them with a long, straight board and shim with thin wedges of wood if necessary.

4 Start working at one edge of the room, cutting tiles, if necessary, to bridge the gap between the backing strip at the wall and the first furring strip. Cut the edges without tongues and place the cut edges toward the walls. Snap a chalk line down the center of the first furring strip to help keep the first row straight.

5 As you install each tile, drive two staples, one directly on top of the other, into each corner of the tile. The first staple will flare the legs of the second and provide better holding power. Don't worry about any minor gaps between edges of the tile field and adjoining walls. They can be covered with cove molding. If necessary, glue the final row of tiles in place.

COVERING OBSTRUCTIONS

1 Hot and cold water pipes are usually ½ inch in diameter, so ordinary furring strips provide enough space for the pipes to fit between the tiles and joists. Plan carefully so the pipes run between the strips. Note the location of any valves or joints that may have to be worked on in the future.

2 Accommodate large pipes by doubling the furring. Attach the first layer to the joists, as shown on the previous page. The second layer of furring runs at a right angle to the first. Major obstructions, such as ceiling beams, can be boxed in with wood, then painted or stained.

FITTING IN RECESSED LIGHTING

1 To avoid lowering the ceiling any more than necessary, install recessed lighting. Square fixtures are designed to fit into the same space as a regular tile. For round fixtures, install the box and wiring according to the manufacturer's directions. Using a razor knife, cut an adjoining tile to fit around the box.

2 Cut the next tile so it, too, fits around the fixture. Because some fixtures get very hot, be sure to follow the manufacturer's recommendations about the size and type of bulbs you can install. If possible, wire the lamp into an existing circuit, but be sure you aren't overloading the circuit. A licensed electrician should handle the wiring of new circuits.

Because it deadens sound so effectively, acoustic tile is well suited to recreation rooms and workrooms in the basement. It is also one of the easiest materials for amateurs to work with. A razor knife and straightedge are the only tools needed.

The 12x12-inch tiles are the most popular, but larger sizes are available. Bigger tiles mean less work, but often they don't fit the scale of small or narrow rooms.

If you have an even ceiling, you can cement or staple acoustic tiles directly to it. You need to put up furring strips only if the ceiling is unfinished (with open joists) or if the finished ceiling is uneven.

INSTALLING A SUSPENDED CEILING

PUTTING UP THE GRID

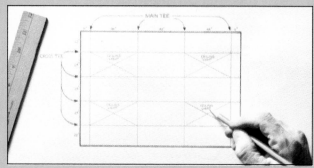

1 Outline the ceiling on graph paper, noting the position of joists, ducts, pipes, and proposed lighting fixtures. Divide the plan into 2x4-foot panels.

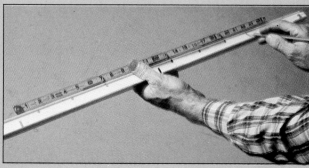

4 Measure and cut the main tees before starting installation. Be careful not to kink the metal as you work with it. Sand any rough edges until smooth.

2 Snap a chalk line on one wall at a right angle to fit the joists. This line represents the finished height of the ceiling. Use wood to bridge openings.

5 Snap chalk lines over joists to mark locations of main tees. Stretch string across the room to locate ceiling level, then hang tees from joist wires.

3 Nail the wall angle along the chalk line. Use masonry fasteners for block or concrete walls. Check the angle for level, and adjust it if necessary.

6 Install the cross tees by laying them 4 feet apart on top of the main tee flanges. Cut cross tees as needed to bridge gaps of less than 2 feet.

Suspended ceilings are popular with do-it-your-selfers, and with good reason. You can install one in a weekend at a cost that will fit into the tightest of budgets. A suspended ceiling has another advantage: It hangs below ductwork and pipes, so you don't have to box them in.

The basics

Suspended ceilings have four major elements. *Wall angles* support the edges of panels at walls. *Main tees* are long strips of metal with a cross section shaped like a capital T. The cross member of the T faces down, forming a pair of flanges that support panel edges. *Cross tees* are laid between the main tees to support the narrow edges of the panels. Finally, you'll need the *panels* themselves, plus light fixtures if you plan to add new lighting to your room.

Ceiling highlights

The main problem in installing a suspended ceiling is getting the grid of tees level, which isn't as difficult as it might appear. As long as the two wall angles are the same height from the floor, you shouldn't have major problems.

Before attaching anything to the walls, however, scan the ceiling for objects hanging below the level of the joists. The duct or pipe farthest beneath the joists sets the height of the ceiling. (If you have to drop the ceiling below 7 feet, consider boxing in obstructions, so the ceiling won't seem to press down on you.)

Allow an extra inch or two below the largest obstruction, then check to make sure your ceiling will clear all other obstructions.

To ensure a level installation, attach the first wall angle at the height you've determined for your ceiling, leveling as you go. Temporarily attach the wall angle on the opposite wall, string mason's twine between the two angles, then use a line level to check the location of the second angle. (A line level is an inexpensive bubble level that hangs on the twine.)

If you install several of these ceiling-level strings, you won't have any problem getting the main tees level. After attaching suspension wires to the joists, slip the wire through the hole in the tee, then slide the tee down until it lightly touches the string. Bend the wire up sharply to hold the tee at the correct level, and twist the excess wire around the wire above the tee.

The box *opposite* takes you step by step through the process of putting up the grid for a suspended ceiling.

Picking panels

Panels come in a variety of sizes, but most people choose the 2x4-foot size. Panels that size are big enough to make preparations go fast, and they integrate well with standard 4-foot fluorescent lighting fixtures. To install them, you simply lift the lightweight panels— angling them slightly so they'll fit up into the grid—and drop them into place. Edge panels cut easily with a sharp knife.

INSTALLING LIGHTING

1 Install the light fixtures before the ceiling panels. Attach brackets to main tees, then screw fixtures to brackets. Follow the manufacturer's directions.

2 Install light shields on the fixtures. In some cases, shields may already be attached. Wire the fixture, and check to see that it is working properly.

3 Slip the diffusion panels into the tees below the fixtures. Then install all full ceiling panels. Finally, cut and install all the remaining panels.

INSULATING A CATHEDRAL CEILING

Although they are beautiful, cathedral ceilings usually don't have enough insulation. You can remedy this problem without a lot of work thanks to a new generation of plastic insulations. Plastic foam insulation comes in lightweight boards that, inch for inch, stop more heat than any other kind of insulation.

Most insulation boards are made of one of three kinds of plastic. Polystyrene, the same material used in disposable coffee cups, is the insulation being installed in the how-to photographs on the opposite page. For more insulating value, you might want to use polyurethane or polyisocyanurate. Both have a higher R-value than polystyrene but cost more.

Caution: One major drawback to plastic foam boards is that they're combustible. Good building practice—and nearly all fire codes—require the boards to be covered with ½-inch gypsum drywall. You can then safely install paneling or other surfaces.

Insulating basics

Prepare the ceiling by first removing all trim from the edges of the room. Use a small pry bar, or take a small nail set and drive the brads holding the trim partway through the wood, then pull off the trim. If you work carefully, you should be able to reuse the trim pieces.

Adhesive will hold the insulation, but you'll need a nailing base for the drywall, and this means putting up furring strips. If your ceiling has exposed beams, you can nail the furring strips between them. Nail directly into structural beams as illustrated on the opposite page. But if the beams are merely decorative, you'll have to locate the rafters and nail the furring to them.

You can pinpoint the ceiling rafters by using a stud finder or by drilling small holes in the ceiling until you meet resistance all the way. (Most rafters are 16 or 24 inches apart.) As you find each rafter, mark its position with a chalk line or a pencil and long straight board.

Find furring strips that are the same thickness as your insulation (generally ¾ inch). Nail the strips into the rafters, centering them on the lines you drew earlier.

Once the furring is in place, putting up the insulation itself goes quickly. To complete the job, follow the instructions on the opposite page.

Decorating schemes

Once you have installed the insulation and covered it with drywall, you're free to add any decorative treatment you like. In the room shown on this page, sheet paneling was installed between exposed beams. The main advantage of paneling—in addition to its aesthetic qualities—is that you don't have to tape and fill the drywall joints. To learn more about choosing and putting up paneling, see pages 48-61. If you prefer to go with drywall as a finished surface, see pages 110 and 111.

CATHEDRAL CEILINGS

1 Use a small pry bar to remove trim molding around the edges of the ceiling. If the walls are likely to be marred by the bar, insert a thin strip of wood behind the bar, or use a nail set to drive trim nails through the molding. Also, temporarily remove any light fixtures that might interfere with the job.

2 Apply a bead of caulk at those points where the ceiling meets an exterior wall. The caulk prevents air from leaking through the joint, a major source of heat loss in most homes. Aerosol acrylic caulk is easy to work with, but be sure the caulk you choose is compatible with the insulation you're using. A dealer can help you select the right sealant.

3 Rip furring strips to the thickness of your insulation. Nail through the strips and existing ceiling material into the rafters. If there are structural beams exposed on the ceiling, nail into them, as shown here. Use ring-shank drywall nails for extra holding power.

4 If necessary, cut the insulation so panels will fit between the furring. Using a caulking gun, apply adhesive to the back of the insulation. Follow the manufacturer's directions to find out where to place the beads of adhesive. Most recommend a combination of perimeter beads and X-shaped beads. Be sure the adhesive you use will work with the type of insulation you select.

5 Lay the insulation boards between the furring strips, then press hard enough to set the insulation firmly into the adhesive. Because the boards are so light, the insulation should stay up without any problems. Cover the boards with drywall, nailing or screwing it to the furring.

6 Once the drywall is in place, tape and finish all joints, or cover the drywall with paneling. Sheet paneling is particularly easy to use. To make the job go faster, buy or rent a brad driver and use brads that match the color of your paneling. Otherwise, fill exposed nailheads with putty. Reapply trim.

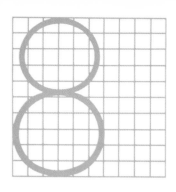

PUT YOUR WALLS AND CEILINGS TO WORK

If your house is like most, it often seems short on storage space. Yet it's probably full of neglected surfaces just waiting for you to use. Look at your walls and ceilings: They have more than enough room to take care of your overstuffed closets, garages, and basement corners. Now look behind your walls at the spaces between the studs. In these normally hidden places, you can store small objects that get lost so easily. Once you realize how roomy your house really is, think about how to stow all that stuff. Drawers aren't the only way. Bins and shelves often work just as well, sometimes better. And when everything is neatly stashed, consider brightening your rooms by "storing" plants on the ceiling.

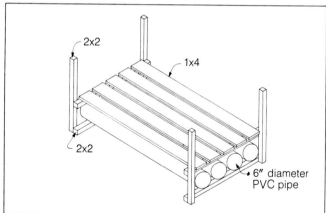

6" diameter PVC pipe

Here's a handy catchall to help organize strips of lumber. Build it from 2x2s with a shelf of 1x4s on top and tubes of 6-inch PVC drain pipe (available at plumbing supply shops) on the bottom. The uprights are 2 feet long, and the crosspieces are 28 inches long. To build it, you'll need 16 feet of PVC pipe, 28 feet of 2x2s, and 20 feet of 1x4s. Build the end frames first. Nail and glue the lap joints, then nail the upper shelf to the frames. Cut the tubes with a hand saw and slide them into place. Glue them together if you like, but the weight will keep them in place. Nail uprights to the joists. To install the catchall parallel to the joists, adjust its width to their spacing. Or nail 2x2s at the bottom of the joists, then attach the catchall.

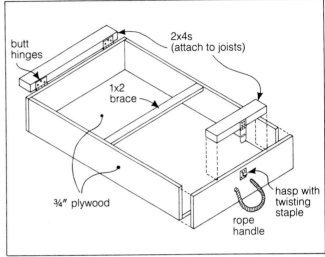

butt hinges

2x4s (attach to joists)

1x2 brace

¾″ plywood

hasp with twisting staple

rope handle

Do you have clutter, clutter everywhere, and no place to put it? Things will improve if you build an overhead storage compartment. Check the ceiling of your garage or basement. You'll probably find an ideal spot to store camping gear, leftover paint, Christmas decorations, out-of-season clothing, and extra bedding for overnight guests. Anything that's light enough to be supported by a couple of butt hinges will stay high and dry in the joist-hung box, *left* and *above*. (For heavier objects, you'll have to use stronger hardware and supports.) If you want to reach something, draw up a stepladder and unlatch the hook.

To build the box, start with ¾-inch plywood cut to the desired dimensions. Nail a 1x2 across the middle for stability, as shown in the plan. Add interior dividers to make separate compartments. Drill holes to fashion a simple rope handle, or screw on a metal drawer pull. When the box is complete, apply a primer to the outside of the plywood, then enamel it for a smooth finish.

To attach the box, nail two 2x4s as anchor boards to the joists. Install two 3-inch butt hinges at one end of the box and a hasp closure with a twisting staple at the opposite end. Allow adequate clearance behind the end of the hinge (a measurement almost equal to the box's depth). That way, the box can swing open to a slightly angled position without all the objects tumbling from it.
(continued)

119

HANGUPS
(continued)

Turning ceilings into storage areas is a valuable way to use extra space in your house. But don't get stuck on strictly utilitarian installations. Ceilings that work too hard can become dull and uninspiring. Here are some appealing but practical ideas to make your ceilings handsome as well as functional.

For example, if you hang your plants so they spread out on all sides, you not only create a beautiful scene to enliven the room, but you may also find a method to conceal distracting structural details.

At *right,* a leafy canopy disguises what used to be a plain chandelier. Pots of trailing vines surround the metal perimeter. An old wagon wheel would work just as well, as would nearly any framework you might devise on your own.

To make watering easier, add a pulley just above the cap (as in the photo) so the plants will come to you.

High ceilings are best for accommodating such hanging arrangements, but in any room you can still devote a clear corner to a lush rack of plants pouring to the floor, as pictured *opposite, right.* (For more about hanging plants from walls, turn to pages 94 and 95; for details on how to attach hooks to ceilings, see pages 130 and 131.)

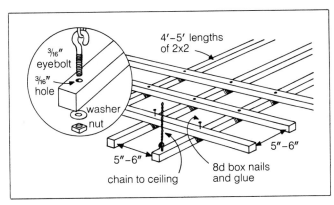

³⁄₁₆″ eyebolt

³⁄₁₆″ hole

washer

nut

4′–5′ lengths of 2x2

5″–6″

5″–6″

chain to ceiling

8d box nails and glue

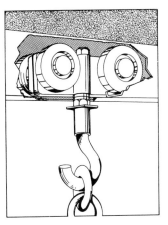

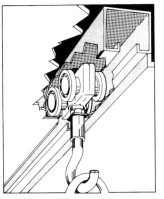

If you've been wishing for a hanging garden like the one *above,* make your wish come true with a garden grid of 2x2s. It will easily support pots from cords and hooks. Just suspend the grid from any part of a ceiling that gets enough natural light. About 4 to 5 feet on each side is a practical size.

The grid shown here nestles in a corner, but you can install a rectangular unit in front of a window or across a narrow room as long as the light is good. Hang the grid with sections of chain from eyebolts screwed into the ceiling.

To make the grid, join the 2x2s with 8d nails and glue, evenly spacing them 5 to 6 inches apart. Keep the pieces square as you nail. As the plan shows, drill ³⁄₁₆-inch holes for eyebolts. Then fasten the grid to them with washers and nuts.

If your plants need more light, as those in the photo do, clamp a few grow-bulb lamps to the grid.

If you like to move plants around or if you want to cover a wall or window, here's a suggestion that will put you on the right track.

In this case, that track is one that normally supports closet doors. You can buy it at most lumberyards. The type shown *above* attaches to blocking between joists and is mortised into the ceiling about an inch, leaving only the lower edge exposed.

If you don't want to bother with recessing a track, look for one that surface-mounts. To make it less obtrusive, paint it to match the ceiling color.

To suspend plants from most types of hanging-door rollers, drill a hole through the center of the carriage assembly and insert a threaded hook. Tighten with nuts above and below the carriage. As you put up more plants, install extra rollers.

SHELVING

Bulk storage, the answer to messy households everywhere, often causes a problem it is supposed to solve: It takes up a lot of space.

That doesn't happen with this shelving. The heavy-duty unit at *right* provides nearly 16 cubic feet of storage without protruding into the room. At the same time, the angled vertical fins cut down on the depth of the shelves and lift the unit off the floor.

Think of what you can do with just one or two narrow modules like this at the end of a hallway. Or try extending the shelf the whole width of a room. Moreover, you can construct shelves of varying depths in the same unit.

You can even make the shelves work doubly hard by installing two tiers, with one shelf extending in front of the other.

To provide strength, each vertical fin is two layers thick. Dowels ⅜ inch thick support the shelves, which can line up on both sides of the fins or sit at varying heights on either side. Keep the shelves short so they won't sag.

Cut the faces of the fins from ½-inch particleboard. Drill dowel holes in all but the two outside pieces. To align the holes, lay out a drilling pattern on one piece, clamp it together with several other panels, and drill through all the layers with a drill press. Make the holes slightly larger than the dowels. Assemble each fin with glue, and nail ½x1½-inch strips of pine to serve as spacers between faces at top, front, and bottom, as shown in the plan at *right*.

Spacers at the back, also ½x1½ inches, serve as mounting strips. Using 3-inch No. 10 or No. 12 wood screws, attach them (with the

½-inch side up) to studs behind the wall surface. Plumb the spacers with a level.

Nail the 1x2 trim to the edges of each fin. Cut the dowels and the shelves, adding 1x2 stiffeners to the front edges of the shelves. Sand all the edges until they're round, then paint the fins to match the walls. If you wish, stain the dowels and shelves a dark color.

To attach the fins to the wall, spread their back edges slightly so they slip over the mounting strips. Secure with screws.

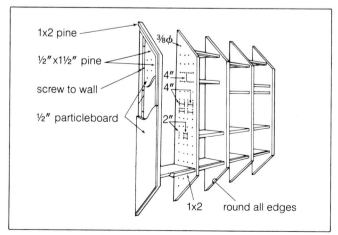

1x2 pine
⅜φ
½" x1½" pine
screw to wall
½" particleboard
4"
4"
2"
1x2   round all edges

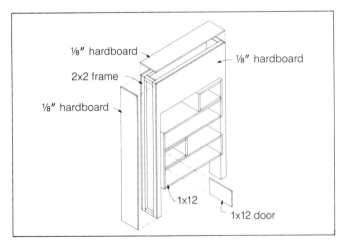

1/8" hardboard

1/8" hardboard

2x2 frame

1/8" hardboard

1x12

1x12 door

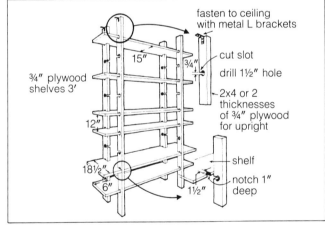

fasten to ceiling
with metal L brackets

cut slot

drill 1½" hole

2x4 or 2
thicknesses
of ¾" plywood
for upright

shelf

notch 1"
deep

¾" plywood
shelves 3'

15"

¾"

12"

18½"

6"

1½"

Divide and conquer with this storage divider that is 6½ feet high, 4 feet wide, and 10 inches deep. To build it, you'll need two 4x8-foot sheets of ⅛-inch hardboard, 30 feet of 1x12s, 36 feet of 2x2s, and a pair of hinges.

Build a frame of 2x2s in a giant, inverted U-shape. Cover the top and ends with ⅛-inch hardboard, then cut big pieces of hardboard into U-shapes to cover the front and back. Also cover the inside of each end with hardboard.

Using the 1x12s, build two 10-inch-high box frames to fit between the ends. Install the boxes by nailing through the ends of the 2x2 frame. Space them about 10 inches apart. The boxes can project on one side only (as in the plan) or on both sides.

Finally, build two 10x15-inch boxes out of 1x12s. Omit the ends on one, enclose the other with a hinged door, and set both boxes in place.

Flexible to handle and easy to build, the take-apart divider *above* holds books, records, and stereo equipment. Use four 2x4s cut to fit from floor to ceiling. Or you can use eight 4-inch-wide strips of ¾-inch plywood, with two cut, glued, and nailed to serve as uprights at each corner. Use an electric drill with a 1½-inch spade bit and a saw to drill holes and cut slots in the upright poles.

Cut the shelves from ¾-inch plywood. Five of them are 15x36 inches, one is 18½x36 inches (deep enough to hold a turntable).

Notch the wide shelf to fit between the uprights. To make the entire unit adjustable, add extra slots at different heights. Fasten uprights to the floor and ceiling with L-shape metal brackets. Allow a 6-inch overhang on shelf ends. Finish the unit by adding edging tape to the shelves and uprights.

(continued)

SHELVING

(continued)

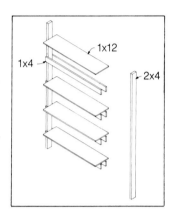

Just right for a garage or basement, shelves like these are a cinch to make and a practical way to put everything in its place.

To build them, use the less expensive grades of lumber or scrap wood you have on hand. For a single 4-foot-wide unit, you'll need 16½ feet of 2x4s (assuming 8 feet from floor to joists), 32 feet of 1x4s, and 16 feet of 1x12s.

Cut two vertical 2x4s, allowing about 3 extra inches at the top so you can nail them to the joists. Pick a spot for the shelves, position the 2x4s, and measure from the outside of one to the outside of the other. This figure will give you the length of the 1x4 shelf supports. Then cut the 1x4s and nail them to the edges of both 2x4s, spaced according to the size of the items you intend to store.

Swing the framework into place and plumb the 2x4s with a level, marking their location on the ceiling joists. Cut 1x12 shelves to fit, center each shelf over the 1x4s, and nail it in place.

Of course, the shelves don't *have* to be next to a wall. In addition, if you decide to build parallel units, you'll need room to move. Allow at least 2 feet between them; 3 feet is better.

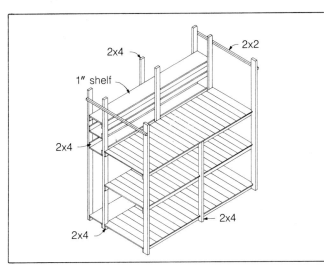

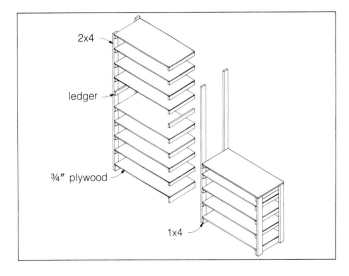

Here's handy storage for luggage, boxes, and leftover lumber. For a 6-foot-wide unit, you'll need 146 feet of 2x4s, 24 feet of 1x12s, 7 to 8 feet of 2x2s, and at least 135 feet of 1x4s for the shelves.

The shelves rest on three big frames that you prefabricate on the floor and tip into place. Start by laying three uprights on the floor, then glue and nail 2x4 ledgers and a 2x4 base piece onto them. Make an identical frame and turn it over on the floor. Glue and nail 2x4 ledgers to the

other side (see plan for middle unit). Make a third frame from three additional uprights, but keep these on edge as you nail on the 2x4 ledgers.

Stand the units in place, then mark the joists and nail 2x2 crosspieces to them. Cut shelf pieces from 1x12s and 1x4s. Anchor the back unit to the joist crosspieces, then anchor the middle unit, using 1x12 shelf pieces as spacers. Do the same with the front unit. Glue and nail on the remaining shelves.

Each shelf *above* holds 77 pint jars or 56 quarts. You'll need three sheets of ¾-inch plywood, 18 feet of 1x4s, and 32 feet of 2x4s.

Cut 2x4-foot pieces from the three sheets of plywood, then saw each remaining 4x6-foot piece into four 2x3-foot shelves. From the 2x4 pieces, saw two shelves, one for the 37½-inch counter top. Cut four 1x4 supports for the bottom shelves, and cut the other 2-inch-wide ledger supports from plywood.

To make the taller set of shelves, build two "ladder"

ends with four 78-inch 2x4s. Space the shelf supports every 8¾ inches. Stand the "ladders" on end, then nail on scrap lumber as temporary supports. Nail in the bottom, top, and one middle shelf.

Remove the temporary holders, and turn the unit face-down. Add a diagonal 1x4 brace to the back, nailing into both the 2x4s and the three shelves.

Build a 36-inch-high "ladder" and connect it to the main unit by nailing in two shelves and the top. Slip in the remaining shelves.

USING STUD SPACE

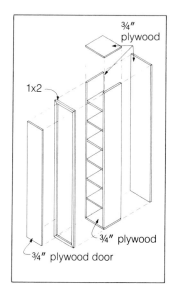

¾"
plywood

1x2

¾" plywood

¾" plywood door

Behind the walls of your house are areas literally studded with space. Before trying to use them, however, check for concealed pipes or wiring in the walls by identifying their locations from the basement or attic.

The bathroom storage unit at *left* fits into the 14½-inch-wide space between two studs. After you cut away the wall's surface, build a five-sided box from ¾-inch plywood. Use butt joints, white glue, and finishing nails. Cut six 6x6 shelves from the ½-inch plywood and nail them in place. Allow 6 inches between shelves.

Cut and apply 1x2 strips to the front; miter the corners. Measure the door opening and cut a ¾-inch plywood door to fit over the top six compartments. Finish it off with plywood edging tape. Hang the door with unobtrusive pivot hinges.

Next, install the toilet-paper holder in the bottom compartment. Attach the pull and catch. Hang the unit in the wall by screwing through the sides into wall studs.

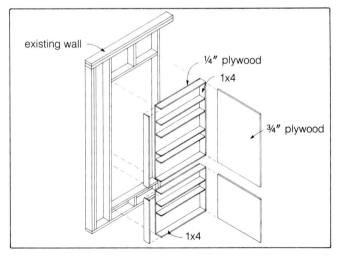

existing wall

¼″ plywood

1x4

¾″ plywood

1x4

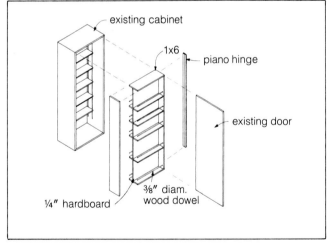

existing cabinet

1x6

piano hinge

existing door

¼″ hardboard

⅜″ diam.
wood dowel

Both of the units shown *above* occupy two stud spaces. To fit them in, you need to cut out the center stud and tie it to the adjacent studs with short lengths of 2x4, as shown in the drawing *above left.*

Cut away the drywall with a saber saw. Carefully saw the middle stud at top and bottom. You'll probably discover that it's attached to drywall on the other side. Slip a hacksaw blade between the stud and drywall and cut any nails or screws. Remove the stud and add the horizontal pieces.

For each unit, build a frame of 1x4s to fit the opening. Add ¼-inch plywood at the back. Install shelves of 1x4s. (You can use 1x6 shelves if you have 6-inch studs or if you don't mind the shelves projecting into the room.)

Nail the units to the studs. Cut two ¾-inch plywood doors and attach to the 1x4 frames with pivot hinges.

A door can also store if you fit it with shelves as shown *above.* Replace a door or tuck an all-new unit between studs.

For the outside frame, cut four 1x6s slightly smaller than the opening. Remove the door and shelves from the cabinet (if any); cut back the shelves to accommodate the unit you'll be building.

To hold the ¼-inch hardboard divider, cut dadoes in the middle of the 1x6 lengths, and drill holes for the dowels. Nail and glue the frame, divider, and dowels.

Cut and install 1x3 shelves on each side of the unit and hang the original door in place.

Finish the job by mounting the swing-out unit with a piano hinge attached to the cabinet frame or stud, or by mounting it on a 2x2 screwed to the stud at the side.

HANGING BASICS

Don't get hung up by the confusing array of objects used to attach things to a wall. The one you choose will depend on two things: the weight of the item you're going to hang and the composition of the wall (plaster and lath, drywall, or masonry). Study the examples on these two pages; they should give you most of the information you need. If you need extra help, check at a hardware or housewares store.

The *ordinary nail* still does a good job of supporting lightweight items. However, as you drive a nail deeper and deeper into a wall, it often creates a bigger and bigger hole. Eventually, it may loosen and even fall out.

If you use *expansion anchors* or *expansion bolts,* be sure to get the right size. They must match the thickness of the wall they're applied to. To check, drill a small test hole.

Fiber, lead, and *plastic anchors,* all small cylinders made from different materials, insert into drilled holes. As you twist in a screw, these anchors expand and grip the wall securely. When you redecorate and want to remove them, tap them into the hollow center of the wall and spackle the hole. Other types of anchors—types generally not recommended for use at home—stay in place so tightly that only demolishing the wall will get them out.

(continued)

ATTACHING TO WALLS

LIGHT OBJECTS

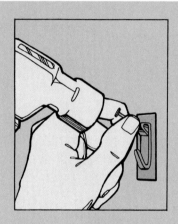

If you're hanging light objects, the easiest attachment to use is an *ordinary picture hook,* sold in hardware stores and most dime stores. It usually holds items weighing up to 20 pounds. If you have plaster walls, nail the hook through a piece of masking tape to prevent the surrounding plaster from crumbling. Two hooks next to each other add strength.

MEDIUM-WEIGHT OBJECTS

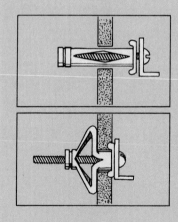

Hollow-wall expansion anchors open behind the surface of the wall as you twist the bolt into place (assuming, of course, that you have drilled the right size hole). Tighten the device with the bolt, then remove the bolt, thread it through the object to be attached, and reinsert. This kind of anchor won't pull loose once the flanges have expanded, but it works only in hollow walls.

HEAVY OBJECTS

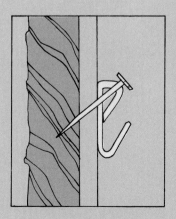

Large picture hooks will support heavy objects if you nail or screw the hook directly into a stud. Locate studs in one of three ways: Tap on the wall until you hear a thud, use a magnet to find the nails in the studs, or examine the baseboards for nails, which are usually driven into studs. Electrical receptacles also are usually nailed to studs.

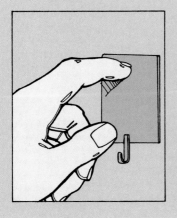

If you want to avoid making holes in the wall, try *gummed picture hooks* on prepared adhesive strips. They support posters, small pictures, and other light objects. Before applying one, be sure the wall is clean and dry. If it isn't, the adhesive won't work. Moisten the patch, position it, and let it dry according to directions. To remove, moisten with warm water, peel off, and clean away adhesive.

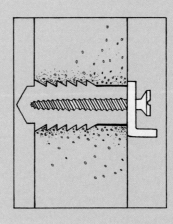

Plastic anchors provide solid support for light or medium-weight objects. Drill the hole and insert the anchor. The screw expands the anchor, causing it to grip firmly. Leave part of the screw exposed so you can hang a picture or other hardware on the wall.

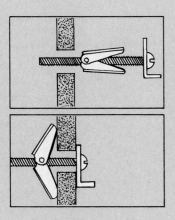

Toggle bolts also expand behind the wall after you insert them into the hole. The wings hold the object firmly against the wall. To insert, put the screw through the object you're hanging, then tighten the device while holding the object in place. Once the wings have expanded, you can't remove the screw without losing the wings behind the wall.

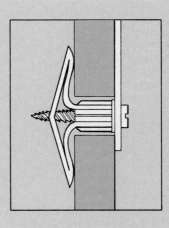

A little-known device, the *plastic toggle anchor* works well in all walls, including brick and concrete. Drill a hole the length of the anchor. Push the flexible wings together before inserting the anchor in the hole. When the front is level with the surface of the wall, insert a nail to pop the wings apart, causing them to grip the wall. Insert a screw and hang the picture.

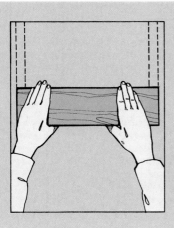

Secure unusually heavy objects by attaching a piece of 1x4 or 1x6 to the wall and bridging the space between two or more studs. Because bridging distributes weight between the studs, you can attach an object anywhere along the wall, not just where the studs are.

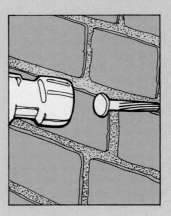

To attach weighty objects to a masonry wall, use specially hardened masonry nails and a heavy hammer. Drive them into concrete block, brick, or mortar joints. Wear goggles to protect your eyes from flying chips. (To hasten the process, you may want to make a small starter hole in the masonry with a carbide-tipped drill.)

HANGING BASICS
(continued)

Hanging objects from the ceiling is like hanging them on the wall, except that you are working directly overhead. You'll be working mostly from a ladder, and usually with a helper, especially when suspending heavy objects.

Most things made to be hung from a ceiling, such as lighting tracks, suspended lamps, and chandeliers, are lightweight and don't pose many problems. Heavier objects, on the other hand, need extra support.

Before hanging anything from a ceiling, do a little homework. Determine the type of ceiling you have and the weight of the object to be hung. Most drywall ceilings safely support up to 50 pounds. Lath-and-plaster ceilings can handle 75 to 100 pounds. From 100 pounds to a limit of 200 pounds, hang everything from a joist.

Concrete presents problems, but once you hang an object, concrete will hold 200 pounds per anchor.

In addition to the suggestions illustrated on these two pages, you may want to try the old-fashioned method of drilling a hole in the concrete ceiling and filling it with a wooden dowel or plug, tightly pushed in. Then screw in an eyehook, as though you were attaching the object to a joist or stud.

A caution: If you have radiant concrete ceilings, *don't* hang anything from them. You are likely to disturb the heating wires and could suffer a serious shock.

ATTACHING TO CEILINGS

LIGHT OBJECTS

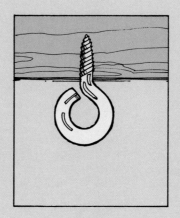

To hang something weighing less than 25 pounds from a plaster ceiling, twist a small screw eye or screw hook into one of the lath boards under the plaster. Even cuphooks will work and may look better. Use a toggle hook in drywall (see *below*)

MEDIUM-WEIGHT AND HEAVY OBJECTS

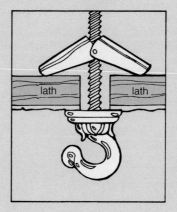

lath   lath

The *toggle bolt* holds medium-weight objects to drywall or lath and plaster. It slips through a hole just big enough for the closed toggles. The special toggle assembly illustrated here includes a swag hook that screws onto the bolt before you insert the toggles. Tighten to secure the whole attachment.

FROM CONCRETE

The *anchor* (made of lead, fiber, or nylon) fits into a hole equal to the anchor's diameter. Drill the hole with a carbide bit. Twist the screw eye or screw hook into the anchor to expand the soft material tightly against the hole. Friction holds it up.

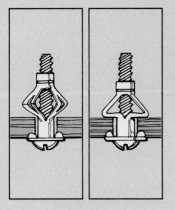

The *expansion anchor* or *expansion bolt* works by expanding, which creates support as you insert the bolt. Once the sleeve expands, you can remove the bolt. To hang an item, replace the bolt with an eyebolt or screw eye.

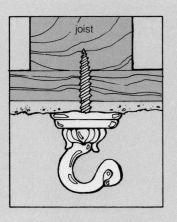

Heavier objects should be suspended directly from joists, rather than from drywall or lath. A strong screw eye or hook twisted straight into a joist works well. To find out how to locate joists, see the box at *right*.

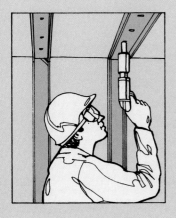

To make the job go fast, rent a *stud gun*. Load it with a pin instead of a bullet, along with a cartridge or charge. Hold it against the ceiling and shoot into the surface. If you're shooting through a steel support, as illustrated here, you'll need a more powerful charge.

LOCATING JOISTS

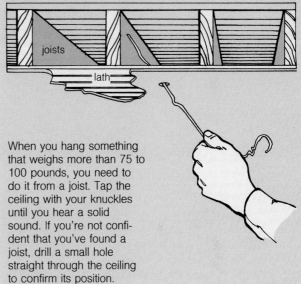

When you hang something that weighs more than 75 to 100 pounds, you need to do it from a joist. Tap the ceiling with your knuckles until you hear a solid sound. If you're not confident that you've found a joist, drill a small hole straight through the ceiling to confirm its position.

Failing this, drill again through the same hole, but at a slant. Insert and rotate a straightened coat hanger until you hit a joist. Keeping your thumb fixed on the hanger, mark the spot on the ceiling that corresponds approximately to the distance the hanger has gone into the ceiling. Then drill a hole for the screw.

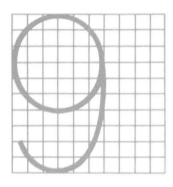

INSULATING AND SOUND-PROOFING

A long, long time ago (but not so long ago that you can't remember), heating and cooling costs were low and owning a home was inexpensive. Insulation certainly wasn't a subject to write books about. Then, energy bills suddenly went through the roof, and the topic of insulation became very popular. It still is. This chapter provides easy-to-follow, money-saving information on how to insulate and soundproof your home, and how to do those jobs right.

HOW MUCH INSULATION DO YOU NEED?

Key questions about insulation are how much do you need and how much can you afford? One way to answer them is by figuring out the "payback period," which is how long it takes to get your money back in lower energy bills. With fuel costs still rising, you might think that any money spent on insulation will be repaid quickly. Not true. Installing insulation is sometimes an expensive affair, so it's important to put your money where it will do the most good in the shortest time.

The tables shown *opposite* will help you pinpoint the best investments for your particular house. If you follow this explanation and work through the accompanying examples, you'll be able to find the answers to those key questions about insulating your home.

The upper table gives individual energy index numbers (energy numbers) for eight different uses of insulation and two uses of storm windows and doors in homes in 20 cities. Under the name of the city is the type of heating and cooling system common in that area. (New York City has two listings, for example.)

The lower table works with the upper table to give you "energy payback numbers"—the energy numbers you'll need to repay an investment in seven years.

The numbers also include the assumption that energy costs will go up 10 percent each year and that money you use from savings to buy insulation will cost 6 percent in lost interest.

When using the tables, keep this formula in mind: If the payback number in the lower table is less than the energy number in the top table, the payback period will be less than seven years. If the payback number is larger than the energy number, the payback period will be more than seven years.

Playing our numbers
Now let's look at a couple of examples. Assume you live in Cleveland. You use gas heat and air conditioning and have some insulation in the house. Note that the energy number in the upper table for ceilings/attics in Cleveland is 2630. Now look at the lower table. The second category in the first column applies because you have less than 3 inches of insulation in the ceiling. Assume that you decide to add R-19 insulation and do the work yourself. In that case, the payback number is 1610, which is a little more than half Cleveland's energy number of 2630. That means you should easily recoup your investment in less than seven years.

Let's take another example. This time assume an oil-heated, air-conditioned home in New York. The front door is solid with no glass. Would it pay to install a storm door?

Look at the first table. The energy number for storm doors in New York is 3290. The lower table shows that adding a storm door to a single exterior door without glass has a payback number of 5380 if you do the work yourself. That new storm door will take nearly 11 years to pay for itself.

Now, compute your own home's energy numbers. Find the city nearest your hometown. If you're in the middle between two cities, pick the one with climate most like your own. The formula provides a handy way to determine the value of your investment.
(continued)

INSULATION PAYOFF INDEX

OH-Oil heat   GH-Gas heat   DE-Direct electric   AC-Air conditioning

ENERGY INDEX APPLICABLE TO:	New York	New York	Wash., D.C.	Cleveland	Chicago	Atlanta	Miami	Memphis	New Orleans	Minneapolis	Kansas City	Dallas	Denver	Phoenix	Seattle	San Francisco	Los Angeles	Boston	Salt Lake City	Omaha	Albuquerque
	GH & AC	OH & AC	GH & AC	GH & AC	GH & AC	GH & AC	DE & AC	DE & AC	GH & AC	GH	GH & AC	GH & AC	GH	GH & AC	OH	GH	GH & AC	OH & AC	GH & AC	GH & AC	GH & AC
Ceilings/ attics	4490	4670	3410	2630	3170	2200	2410	2160	1850	3300	1920	2070	1610	2170	3480	1160	710	4500	1980	2240	2240
Ducts in attics	5410	5600	4020	2980	3760	2870	3870	2770	2720		2390	2850	1830	3210			870	4860	2350	2560	2680
Exterior frame walls (wood, brick siding)	4260	4440	3260	2550	3020	2040	2050	2010	1630		1800	1880	1550	1910			670	4410	1880	2160	2120
Storm windows or triple glass	3800	3980	2950	2380	2730	1710	1320	1700	1200		1570	1490	1440	1400			600	4230	1700	2010	1900
Storm doors*	3100	3290	2490	2120	2290	1210	230	1250	540		1220	910	1280	620			480	3970	1420	1770	1570
Floors over vented crawl spaces*	3100	3290	2490	2120	2290	1210	230	1250	540		1220	910	1280	620			480	3970	1420	1770	1570
Walls of unvented crawl spaces*	3100	3290	2490	2120	2290	1210	≤230	1250	540		1220	910	1280	620			480	3970	1420	1770	1570
Ducts in vented crawl spaces	4260	4440	3260	2550	3020	2040	2050	2010	1630		1800	1880	1550	1910			670	4410	1880	2160	2120
Walls of basements*	3100	3290	2490	2120	2290	1210	230	1250	540		1220	910	1280	620			480	3970	1420	1770	1570
Ducts in basement	5410	5600	4020	2980	3760	2870	3870	2770	2720	3300	2390	2850	1830	3210	3480	1160	870	4860	2350	2560	2680

*Energy index is for heating season only—air conditioning effect is negligible.

For a payback in seven years, I will need an energy index number of at least:

If I have:	And I want to:	If I do it myself	If I contract the work
No existing ceiling insulation	Add R-19 ceiling insulation	310	500
	Add R-30 ceiling insulation	390	630
Less than 3" of existing ceiling insulation	Add R-11 insulation	1340	2150
	Add R-19 ceiling insulation	1610	2580
	Add R-30 ceiling insulation	2120	3400
1" attic duct insulation	Add additional 1" duct insulation	1210	2420
More than 1" duct insulation	Add additional 1" duct insulation	2240	4480
Uninsulated exterior walls	Fill cavity with blown or foamed insulation	No	2960
Single exterior windows	Add storm windows	1930	2890
Double (insulating glass) windows	Add storm windows	3520	5270
Single exterior doors with glass	Add storm doors	3750	5360
Single exterior doors without glass	Add storm doors	5380	8070
Floors over vented crawl spaces with no floor insulation	Add R-11 floor insulation	830	1330
	Add R-19 floor insulation	2220	3560
Unvented crawl spaces—no wall or floor insulation	Add R-11 wall insulation	1740	2790
	Add R-19 wall insulation	4510	7220
Uninsulated ducts in vented crawl spaces	Add 1" duct insulation	3030	6050
	Add 2" duct insulation	3580	7160
Bare basement walls two feet or more above exterior grade	Add R-3 wall insulation	1730	2590
	Add R-11 wall insulation	3860	5780
Uninsulated ducts in basements	Add 1" duct insulation	2200	4400
	Add 2" duct insulation	2580	5160

HOW MUCH INSULATION DO YOU NEED?

(continued)

If you add insulation to your home, the money you save will depend on the climate, the level of insulation already in your home, and the cost of energy. Studies show that upgrading an older house that has inadequate insulation can reduce energy consumption by 50 percent. Upgrading a newer, partially insulated home may mean savings of 20 to 30 percent.

Know what you have

Before rushing out to buy insulation, find out how much you already have. The illustration *below right* shows those areas in your home most likely to need extra insulation.

The easiest place to begin your survey is the attic. Use a ruler to measure the depth of the insulation in an unfinished attic. It may be stapled to rafters or laid between floor joists. Take care not to compact it. Using the chart on the opposite page, determine its R-value per inch, then compute the total R-rating. Repeat the process in the area over any unheated crawl space or basement.

Inspecting walls is a bit tougher. Remove the switch plate from an outlet, and peek into the wall cavity with a flashlight. Or make a small hole and patch it. If you see any insulation, your house is probably in pretty good shape. If it is not, insulating a finished wall is best left to a professional (see pages 140 and 141).

In any event, don't poke with sharp objects; you may puncture a vapor barrier. Made from kraft paper, foil, or polyethylene, vapor barriers stop moisture from seeping into the insulation (wet insulation has little R-value). If you have vapor barriers, they should be facing heated areas—directly under floors, walls, and ceiling coverings.

Find your R-value

The map at *right* shows the minimum recommended amounts of insulation for each region of the country. Levels of insulation are measured in units called R-values, which represent the ability of a material to resist the flow of heat. "R" stands for resistance to heat transfer. R-values differ for each type of insulation. The higher the R-value, the better the material's resistance to the flow of heat.

Almost any building material —wood, masonry, fiberboard sheathing, even glass—has some resistance to the transfer of heat. R-values for these materials differ only slightly from one house to another. All you have to do is determine the type of insulation you have, if any, and how much of it. Insulation is rated by inches of thickness. To determine a material's total R-value, multiply the thickness of the insulation by its R-value per inch. Recommended R-values for your climate will help determine how much more insulation you need (see map *above right*).

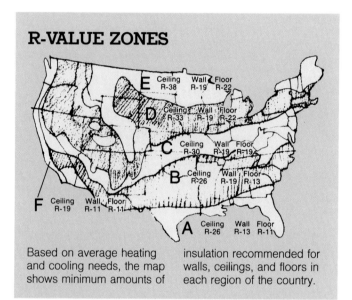

R-VALUE ZONES

Based on average heating and cooling needs, the map shows minimum amounts of insulation recommended for walls, ceilings, and floors in each region of the country.

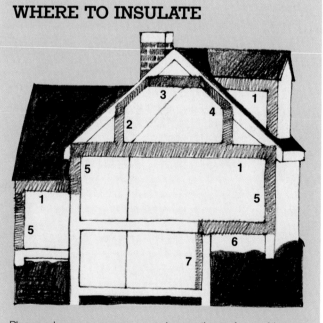

WHERE TO INSULATE

Places where you may need insulation are: (1) ceilings and unfinished attic floors, including dormer ceilings, (2) knee walls in a finished attic, (3) between attic collar beams, (4) sloping sections of a roof in a finished attic, (5) exterior walls, (6) floors above cold crawl spaces, over a porch or unheated garage, (7) the outside walls of heated basements.

YOUR INSULATION OPTIONS

TYPE OF INSULATION	R-VALUE PER INCH THICKNESS	USES	METHOD OF INSTALLATION
BATTS			
Fiber glass	3.0	Unfinished attic floors, rafters, crawl spaces, walls, ceilings	Lay in or friction-fit
Rock wool	3.0		
BLANKETS			
Fiber glass	3.1	Unfinished attic floors, rafters, crawl spaces, walls, ceilings	Staple or adhesive
Rock wool	3.0		
LOOSE FILL—POURED			
Fiber glass	3.1-3.3	Unfinished attic floors; wall or cavity fill	Pour in to required depth
Rock wool	3.0-3.3		
Cellulose	3.7-4.0		
Vermiculite	2.0-2.6		
Perlite	2.0-2.7		
LOOSE FILL—BLOWN			
Cellulose	3.1-4.0	Finished ceilings, walls, floors; cavity fill	Blow into interior cavities
Fiber glass	2.8-3.8		
Rock wool	2.8-3.8		
RIGID			
Extruded polystyrene	4.0-5.4	Roofs, ceilings, walls, foundations; commonly used in basements	Adhesive
Polyurethane	6.7-8.0		
Polyisocyanurate	4.0-4.3		

INSULATING ATTICS

Insulating your home will mean lower energy bills and better living. If both are comforting thoughts, it's time to turn those thoughts into action. Start at the top—in your attic. Because warm air rises, uninsulated or poorly insulated attics allow valuable energy to slip away quickly, more quickly than any other spot in the house. If you button up your attic first, things will begin to improve immediately.

All attics aren't created equal. The way you insulate yours will depend on whether it is finished.

Unfinished attics

In an unfinished attic that you do not intend to use as living space, place insulation in the floor (or add to it) to prevent losing heat from the rooms below. In spots such as this, use batts, blankets, or loose-fill insulation. Batts, made of fiber glass or rock wool, usually come with vapor barriers attached. Spread loose-fill insulation between joists, but add a vapor barrier first.

If you're working in an unfinished attic that has no floor, take some precautions. Install temporary lighting so you can see what you're doing, and place boards across the floor joists to use as a walkway.

Finished attics

In a finished attic or in one you plan to finish, use blankets, batts, or loose-fill insulation.

If the attic ceiling is open, add rigid insulation, which consists of boards made from extruded polystyrene, urethane, or fiber glass. Nail the boards to the undersides of the exposed roof deck, using large-head, galvanized nails. (Roofing nails work well.) Nail on 8-inch centers in both directions, penetrating the wood at least 1¼ inches. Take care not to puncture the roof.

Because much rigid insulation is combustible, *be sure* to cover it with gypsum board before you put up paneling or other materials.

STEPS TO A SNUG ATTIC

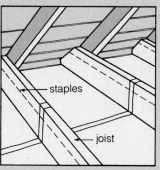

Add a vapor barrier when pouring loose-fill insulation or when installing unfaced batts or blankets on the attic floor. Use 2-mil polyethylene, smoothing it in place between and over the floor joists. Staple with care, and mend any tears in the barrier with tape. (A vapor barrier should always face the living area.)

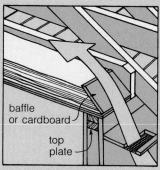

Adequate ventilation is important. Don't block eave vents when you install insulation. Extend it far enough to cover the top plate, but stop batts or blankets short of the vents. If you pour loose-fill insulation, install baffles.

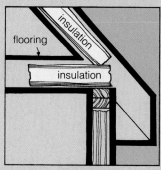

When adding insulation to both walls and floors, try to create a continuous barrier so heat doesn't seep out at the eaves. Use a long stick to push batts into position. Cover the top plate with insulation, and keep it under wiring wherever possible.

If you install blankets in the attic floor, unroll the insulation and cut it to the desired length. Press the blankets between the floor joists, then staple them to the inside of the joists, spacing staples every 6 to 8 inches.

vapor
barrier

drywall

vapor
barrier

batts
in place

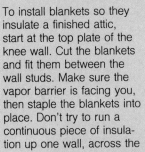

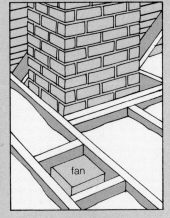

fan

Keep insulation away from recessed light fixtures and exhaust fans. Covering them may create a fire hazard. Instead, build baffles to keep the insulation at least 3 inches away from any motors or fixtures.

If you use loose-fill insulation in an attic floor, pour it between the joists to the desired depth. (Line the floor first with a vapor barrier.) Level the insulation with a wood slat or a rake as you work.

If your attic floor already has some insulation, use *unfaced* batts or blankets (those with no vapor barriers attached). But if the floor is uninsulated, install *faced* batts or blankets. Be sure the vapor barriers point toward the heated areas below.

To install blankets so they insulate a finished attic, start at the top plate of the knee wall. Cut the blankets and fit them between the wall studs. Make sure the vapor barrier is facing you, then staple the blankets into place. Don't try to run a continuous piece of insulation up one wall, across the collar beam, and down the other side. Instead, use three separate pieces, overlapping the vapor barriers. If you use batts of unfaced insulation in a finished attic, cut them longer than required and wedge them into the stud space. Add a vapor barrier of polyethylene film.

INSULATING FLOORS

After you insulate the attic, lower your sights and examine another energy-waster at floor level: your home's crawl space or basement. Once these areas are properly insulated, you'll warm up considerably. You can do both jobs yourself; they usually don't require the services of a professional.

BUNDLING UP UNHEATED SPACES

1 Insulate the floors over unheated areas by working from below—in the basement, crawl space, or garage. You'll need batts or blankets of insulation, a tape measure, a heavy-duty staple gun and staples, wire mesh or chicken wire, shears to cut the wire, and a knife to cut the insulation. Staple the chicken wire or mesh to the bottom of the floor joists, then slide in blankets of insulation, working with small sections, vapor barrier up. Or you can use the method shown at *left*. Wedge batts or blankets into the space between floor joists. The insulation will temporarily stay in place without support.

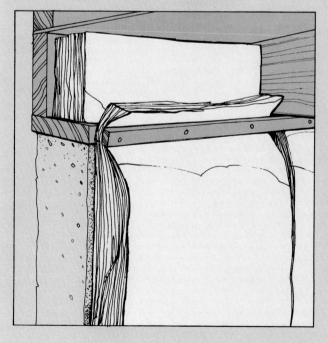

3 For the walls in a crawl space, use batts or blankets. You'll need a sharp knife, tape measure, hammer, nails, furring strips or nailers, and gloves. Where joists run at right angles to the wall, tuck in small sections of insulation against the header. Cut longer pieces and attach them to the sill with furring strips, as shown at *left*. Extend insulation down the wall and 2 feet along the ground. Where joists run parallel to the wall, use longer pieces of insulation and nail them directly to the band joist.

2 Beginning at one end, tack the wire mesh or chicken wire across the floor joists, as shown at *left*. Staple or nail one roll at a time in place, making sure the insulation fits snugly up to the band joist and overlaps the bottom plate. To do the same job, you can cover exposed joists with rigid urethane, polystyrene, or fiber-glass boards. Apply them with adhesive to the joists. Check the local building code to find out whether you need to cover the insulation with a fire-resistant material such as gypsum board. If the joists are covered, as they are in a finished garage ceiling, your best bet is to blow in loose-fill insulation.

4 After you install the insulation, lay a vapor barrier of 6-mil polyethylene on the ground, tucking it under the batts to the foundation wall. Tape the joints of the vapor barrier or lap them at least 6 inches. Finally, secure the polyethylene and insulation with rocks or 2x4 studs, as illustrated at *left*.

HOW TO INSULATE A CONCRETE FLOOR

An uninsulated concrete floor in the basement gives the rest of your house the cold shoulder. The chill may be good for a wine cellar, but it's definitely no way to lower your heating bills. If the first floor of your house is cool, despite a well-insulated attic and adequate weather stripping around windows and doors, the culprit may be the concrete below. If you use the basement for living space, it's even more important to warm a cold floor.

Concrete floors are especially challenging because you obviously can't place insulation beneath them, where it would be most effective. However, there are two approaches that work. (Check local building codes before you try either to be sure they meet standards.)

From the outside

One solution is to wrap the outside of foundation walls in a layer of insulation. To do it, first dig a trench down to the frost line. Then apply 2-inch-thick foam planks from the lowest edge of the siding to the bottom of the trench.

Clearly, this isn't an easy task. Before tackling the job, consult a professional contractor or someone skilled at installing insulation. In fact, you may want to hire a professional to do it for you.

On the other hand, you may discover that you can increase the R-value by insulating the floor itself instead of the foundation wall. In that case, you'll need to install "sleepers."

Sleeper installation

To insulate a concrete floor using this method, glue down wood sleepers, which are 2x4s or boards laid directly over a masonry floor. The sleepers serve as nailers for plywood, strip, or plank flooring.

Before beginning, use a waterproofing compound to seal the floor against moisture. Then lay a vapor barrier of polyethylene on the concrete.

Next, fasten the sleepers at 16-inch intervals. Secure them with masonry nails and adhesive.

Cut rigid foam insulation to fit between the sleepers, and lay the pieces in place.

Finally, lay new subfloor, and finish with the flooring material of your choice.

Whether your basement is heated or unheated, the addition of insulation around the perimeter or on top of the concrete slab should help reduce your heating costs and help stave off the winter chill that has been seeping into your home.

INSULATING WALLS

If you're up against a wall that needs insulation, don't despair. It's possible to blow or to spray insulating materials into finished exterior walls without ripping up those on the interior.

However, doing so is difficult and expensive. In all likelihood, you'll need the services of a contractor who has special equipment and experience to do the job properly. (Partly for these reasons, if your walls already have some insulation, it might not be economical to add to it.)

If you decide to go ahead, search carefully for a reputable professional. Try to get a number of written bids specifying R-values, the amount of insulation required, and the overall cost of the job. In a properly insulated, standard 2x4 wall, you can reasonably expect R-8 for fiber glass or rock wool, R-10 for cellulose (both are blown in; see information at *right*), and R-11.5 for foam.

(One note of caution: Don't use urea formaldehyde foam when insulating any area of the house. Recent studies suggest that the formaldehyde gas given off by the insulation can cause health problems. In fact, the sale of urea formaldehyde foam has been banned by the U.S. Consumer Product Safety Commission. If you want the advantage of foam's higher R-value, use another kind, such as urethane.)

Don't let insulating basement walls get you down. Installing boards of rigid insulation and fitting in soft batts or blankets are two useful methods. The one to use depends partly on where you live and partly on how much room you're willing to take up with the installation.

THREE ALTERNATIVES

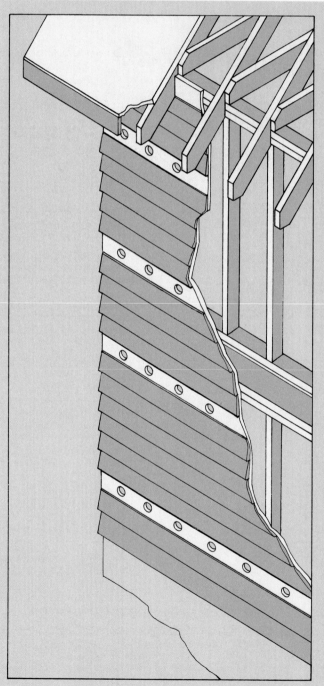

To install insulation in a finished wall, a contractor must reach all the spaces between studs in the wall cavity. For each space, the contractor removes the siding (he doesn't have to strip the entire wall) and drills holes, usually in the sheathing of the outside wall, as shown at *left*. Don't worry about all the drilling. A good contractor will leave no traces when the job is completed.

If the home has a brick-veneer exterior, the same procedure is followed, except that it may be less expensive to do it from the inside of the wall.

(Blowing insulation into a vertical space more than 4 feet high requires what is called the double-blow method. In this case, the contractor cuts two access holes for each stud.)

After drilling the holes, the contractor checks the spaces with a plumb bob, looking for obstructions below the hole. Then special equipment blows the insulation under air pressure through a large, flexible hose into the spaces between the studs.

If the contractor is using foam, it is pumped through a hose with an applicator. With both methods, each wall space is completely filled. When the insulation is in place, the holes are covered with a retainer or plug and the siding is replaced.

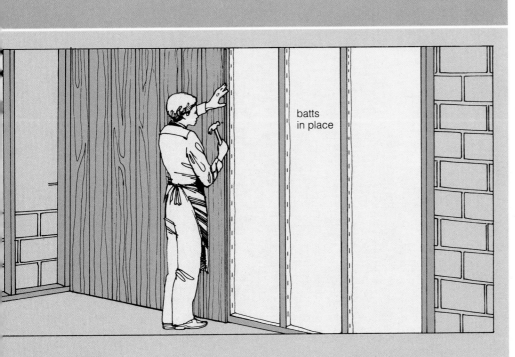

batts
in place

In regions with mild winters, a rating of R-7 is sufficient. In colder areas, you'll need a minimum of R-11.

To reach either value using batts or blankets, you first have to frame out 2x3 or 2x4 stud walls over the top of the masonry. Then staple the soft insulating material, vapor barrier facing you, between the studs of the new built-out walls. Don't be stingy with the staples; drive one every 10 or 12 inches. To finish, cover the studs with drywall or paneling.

Using rigid-board insulation allows the new wall to be as thin as possible, thereby saving space in your basement. Line the walls with furring (to attach the finished wall material), then glue up or tuck in boards between it. (Rigid insulation often comes with an adhesive already applied.)

Because much rigid insulation is combustible, cover it with a minimum of ½-inch drywall, even if you plan to install wood or hardboard paneling later.

Before starting either project, dry up your basement if it is wet. Moist insulation has no value at all. However, don't be concerned by mild condensation. The insulation and vapor barrier usually will solve that problem.

Insulation becomes less important below ground level. Although insulating walls to their full height will provide benefits, you might decide to save money by insulating only down to ground level.

Frame a stud wall in the basement by nailing the bottom plate to the floor and the top plate to the joists. Nail in studs 18 or 24 inches on center. Tuck in batts or blankets between the studs, vapor barrier facing you, and staple them securely. Apply gypsum wallboard or paneling over the insulation, as shown.

If you don't want to frame in a stud wall, use rigid boards to insulate basement walls. With masonry nails, attach furring strips to the walls and around windows and doors. Cut the insulation to fit, and apply it directly to the wall with mastic. Then cover the insulation with at least ½-inch-thick drywall.

SOUNDPROOFING
A ROOM

Common household noise can be irritating. Power tools, dryers, dishwashers, kitchen blenders, and other noisemakers disturb the peace in nearly every American home. Putting your head under a pillow or plugging your ears isn't the answer. You can't eliminate all the noise from your life, but you can reduce its impact. By combining common sense with commonly available materials, you can sound-condition or even soundproof your rooms.

Although your home may not be as noisy as a factory, the jarring effect of household sounds can put you in a bad temper or give you a headache. Those reasons alone are enough to make you want to put a damper on the noise in your home.

Start with the basics. Use earplugs when you're working with noisy power tools. Shut windows and doors to keep out the din of passing traffic. Apply weather stripping if needed, and add double-pane or storm windows to reduce noise from the outside. Landscape the grounds to block and absorb sounds by strategically locating trees, berms, and shrubs.

Indoors, caulk all gaps and cracks with acoustic sealant. Use solid-core doors, acoustic tile, and soft surfaces (fabric, carpeting, draperies) wherever noise is a problem.

The resistance of a wall or floor to the passage of sound is rated by its sound transmission class (STC). The higher the STC value, the better a wall or floor blocks out sound.

A rating of 45 is a good level for walls or floors. New or improved insulation can help control sound dramatically. An uninsulated stud wall covered with gypsum board has an STC rating of only 32, but a staggered stud wall with 1½ inches of insulation and ½-inch gypsum wallboard has an STC rating of 49.

Add fiber-glass or mineral wool insulation to stud walls. On masonry walls, apply rigid polystyrene board insulation over furring strips, then cover with ½-inch drywall.

QUIET WALLS AND DOORS

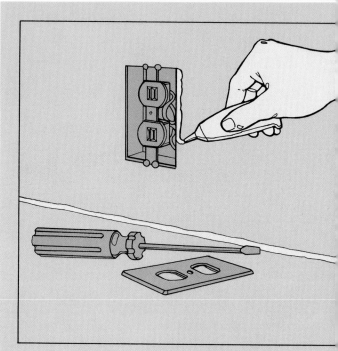

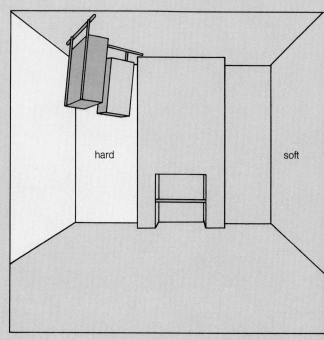

hard

soft

Start your attack on noise with the least expensive solutions, then move on to more costly steps if needed. First, pinpoint the source of noise and try to muffle it there, using carpeting, heavy draperies, and acoustic or cork tiles. Next, try caulking to block the transmission of sound from one room to another. If you're building a new wall, apply nonhardening acoustic caulk under the plates, at tops and bottoms of drywall panels, and around all receptacles. If you're trying to button up existing walls, remove the molding around the ceiling and baseboards and take off the outlet covers. Then apply an acoustic sealant as shown at *left*. Weatherstripping windows also will help keep out noise.

Effectively combining soft and hard materials is a simple way to control sound from loudspeakers. Fabric, carpets, and drapes absorb sound well; wood, metal, and tile do not. Try the system shown at *left*. Apply semigloss paint or adhesive-backed vinyl to plasterboard walls on the "hard" sides of the room to bounce sound. Then cover opposite walls and ceilings with soft, sound-absorbing materials such as carpet, draperies, or fabric. The music will sound better and will be less audible in adjoining areas.

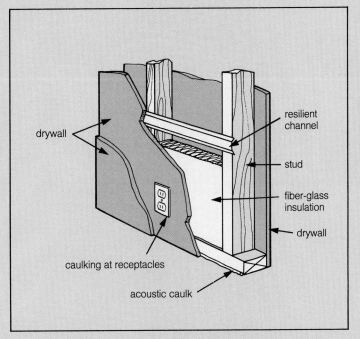

drywall

resilient channel

stud

fiber-glass insulation

drywall

caulking at receptacles

acoustic caulk

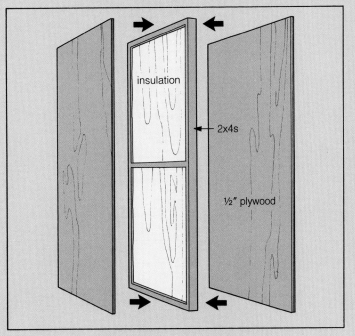

insulation

2x4s

½" plywood

Most wood-stud interior walls don't insulate sound well. The ones that do are built for the job. The drawing at *left* shows an engineered system that substantially reduces the transmission of sound. It uses a double layer of drywall applied over 2x4 wood studs, fiber-glass insulation, and resilient metal channels. For even better results, stagger 2x4 studs to create a 2x6 wall cavity, then weave the insulation between the studs horizontally. Finish with drywall. Adding any insulation to the walls will help make a room quieter and cozier.

If you invest a few extra dollars in a solid-core door and add weather stripping around the door frame, you'll help keep sound from leaving the room. To make a quiet door, follow the drawing at *left*. Cut four 8-foot 2x4s to fit the doorway, allowing ½ inch for new carpet or weather stripping. Next, assemble the 2x4s, as shown, then glue and nail one sheet of ½-inch plywood to the 2x4 frame. Stuff and staple insulation in place. Glue and nail the second sheet of plywood to the other side. Hinge the door so it opens into the room, then apply self-stick weather stripping.

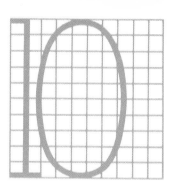

CARING FOR WALLS AND CEILINGS

Fingerprints, holes from picture hangers, little cracks that beg to be filled, moisture in the basement. Even the best of wall and ceiling surfaces demand attention from time to time. This chapter tells how to cope with everyday inevitabilities as well as how to repair more serious damage to plaster, drywall, paneling, and ceramic tile. With a little know-how you can maintain your walls and ceilings in A-1 condition.

MAINTAINING WALLS AND CEILINGS

Most cleaning and repair jobs take only a few minutes. The problem is getting around to them. If you tend to procrastinate, use your "putting-off" time to plan what you're going to do about a problem when you finally get the urge to tackle it.

When you notice a stain on the wall or a scratched wood panel, jot down what's wrong and where, along with any cleaning agents or tools you need (see chart, *opposite*). After several small jobs have accumulated, you can deal with them all at once, armed with the necessary aids.

A stock of "spare parts" saves time and effort. Extra paneling, wall covering, or paint purchased with your original order assures a good match for future repairs.

Following are some guidelines for keeping your walls and ceilings shipshape.

Paneling
Before applying anything other than a dustcloth, make sure the treatment is suited to the type of paneling. As discussed in Chapter 3, most paneling is made of either plywood or processed wood fiber, overlaid with either genuine wood veneer, vinyl or paper that simulates wood grain, or in the case of waferboard, thin slices of real wood with no overlay. All of these can be cleaned with a cleaner manufactured for the specific type. Avoid abrasives, which can scratch or dull the finish. Do not try to spot-sand and refinish because the repaired spot will not blend in, and with overlays, you'll be down to bare wood with no grain. Always test any solution in a small, unobtrusive spot before applying it to large surfaces.

Plaster/drywall
Follow cleaning guidelines in the chart *opposite*. Keep a small jar of paint in a handy place for fast touch-up jobs that stretch the time until another all-over coat is needed.

Wall coverings
As with paneling, tailor the care to the wall covering you have (washable, scrubbable, or non-washable). Loose edges of most types can be reglued with white paste. Use vinyl adhesive or white glue for vinyl wall coverings.

Slit across bubbles and blisters with a sharp razor blade (follow the pattern lines). Lift the corner, apply paste or glue, and press back in place. Sponge off extra adhesive before it dries.

Large holes, tears, and stains can be patched with a scrap of matching wall covering (from your stock of "spare parts"). Tear the edges of the patch so it will be less noticeable, and glue over the damaged area.

Acoustic tiles and panels
Gently clean with a damp sponge and a mild detergent solution. Resist the urge to use a mop on the ceiling, because the material is soft and dents easily. Lay-in panels should be removed from the grid for cleaning. Acoustic ceilings can be painted, but too many coats will clog the pores and affect sound absorption. Manufacturers recommend no more than three coats of a "non-bridging" paint.

CLEANING WALLS AND CEILINGS

	REGULAR CARE	SPOT AND STAIN REMOVAL	SPECIAL TREATMENT
PANELING			
Solid wood/wood veneer	Dust smooth surfaces with soft cloth; rough surfaces with vacuum cleaner brush attachment. Clean with mild detergent solution or a cleaner-polisher made expressly for wood paneling.	If mild detergent and cleaner fail, try rubbing with a rag saturated with solvent. Test first. If solvent cleans without damaging wood, proceed. If shine is dulled, restore with paste wax and buff.	Use paste wax, the meat of an oily nut, a crayon-like touch-up stick, or wood stain to repair scratches and small gouges. Don't attempt to spot-sand and refinish.
Vinyl/printed wood grain	Same instructions as above, but use only those cleaners specified as safe for synthetic and plasticized surfaces.	Try heavy-duty liquid or spray cleaner recommended for painted walls. Rinse thoroughly and buff the surface dry. Do not use strong solvents.	Fill scratches and small holes with crayon touch-up stick. Blend surface scratches with stain.
PLASTER/DRYWALL			
	Dust with cloth-covered broom or vacuum cleaner brush attachment. Wash with mild detergent solution or use commercial wall cleaner.	Use degreaser on oily spots and stains.	If finish must be renewed, clean first before repainting. Seal spot repairs with primer or shellac before painting.
WALL COVERINGS			
	Dust with wall mop or soft cloth tied to broom. Work from ceiling down. Use vacuum cleaner brush attachment on flocked wall coverings to prevent shedding or matting.	Use degreaser on oily spots and stains. The washable and scrubbable types can take mild detergent solution or special foam cleaner. Avoid abrasive cleaners and steel wool.	Use dough-type wallpaper cleaner on non-washable wall coverings.
ACOUSTIC TILE			
	Dust with cloth-covered broom or vacuum cleaner brush attachment. Use mild detergent solution on washable types.	Use detergent solution on greasy spots and stains.	Vinyl or painted acoustic ceilings can be repainted with a thin coat of latex paint to renew appearance. Use dough-type wallpaper cleaner on unpainted surfaces or on finishes that cannot be painted.

REPAIRING PLASTER AND DRYWALL

REPAIRING PLASTER WALLS

SPACKLING HAIRLINE CRACKS

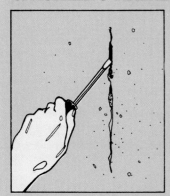

1 Widen the crack to about ⅛ inch by running a thin blade up and down the fissure. You'll give your repair extra strength if you dig out the crack about an inch past each end. Blow out loose plaster.

2 Rub the crack with a fingerful of spackling compound, pressing it into the opening. Force the filler in as deep as you can. You may need to repeat this after an hour or so. When the patch is dry, lightly sand and seal with primer before painting. Without this primer coat, the repair might bleed through to the finish coat of paint.

PATCHING LARGE CRACKS

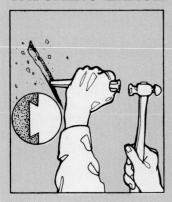

1 Undercut the crack to make it broader underneath than on the surface. This "keys" the space and keeps filler in place. Mix a small batch of patching plaster or use premixed joint compound. If you use plaster, thoroughly wet the crack just before patching to ensure a secure bond.

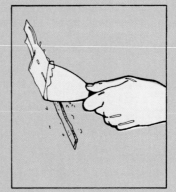

2 Pack patching material into crack with a putty knife or wide-blade taping knife. After 24 hours make a second application to level off the repair. If you use plaster, wet the area first. When the second coat is dry, smooth with fine sandpaper or a damp sponge. Seal with primer before painting.

If your home has plaster walls, you must expect to do a certain amount of filling. Some cracks—usually the harmless ones that run from corners, doors, and windows —will return no matter how many times you fill them.

Watch for loose and crumbly cracks, holes, and bulges. They often indicate a leak somewhere.

You can use plaster to fill cracks and holes, but too much or too little water in the original mix weakens the patch. That's why premixed materials are a better choice for small repairs.

• *Spackling compound* is good for filling hairline cracks, holes from picture hooks, and other small blemishes.

• *Drywall joint compound* works well in all but the finest cracks. It fills fairly deep holes with a couple of applications.

• *Patching plaster* must be mixed, but it is stronger than other fillers. Use it to fill large holes and cracks.

Drywall

Drywall (also known as gypsum board or plasterboard) is made of large sheets of pressed gypsum faced on both sides with heavy paper. These sheets are attached to studs with glue, nails, or screws. The joints between the sheets are covered with perforated paper tape and are smoothed over with joint compound, giving the appearance of an uninterrupted surface.

Most drywall repairs don't require special equipment, and can be made with premixed compound, a roll of tape, a broad taping knife, and ordinary hand tools.

REPAIRING DRYWALL

FILLING DENTS

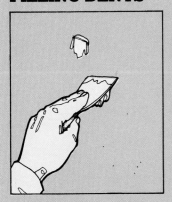

1 Sand the depression to roughen its surface so filler will adhere well. Pack the area with joint compound. A second coat might be needed if the patch shrinks while it is drying. Blend the patch with its surroundings with a light sanding or by wiping with a dampened sponge.

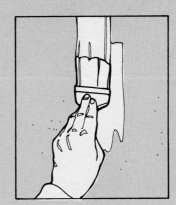

2 Prime the filled area. Because joint compounds are relatively porous, you need to cover the patch with sealer or shellac to prevent the absorption of paint. Some paints serve as primers.

MENDING SPLIT TAPE

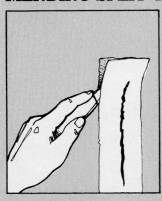

1 Use a sharp knife to gently lift the loose tape from the drywall. Cut carefully at the edges or you may pull off material from either side of the tape.

Smooth rough spots with fine sandpaper. Apply joint compound to the wall surface and position new tape. Smooth out bubbles with light, vertical knife strokes.

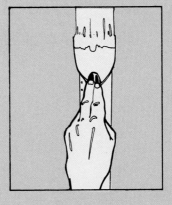

2 While compound is still wet, apply a second coat to surface. Let dry, then lightly coat again, feathering out the edges. Sponge or sand when dry to give a smooth surface.

SETTING POPPED NAILS

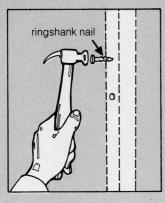

ringshank nail

1 Press the drywall panel against the stud, then drive new nails above and below the popped one. Ring-shank nails hold best.

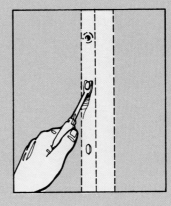

2 "Dimple" each nail below the surface with your last hammer blow. Pull the popped nail (or drive below surface) and fill dimples with compound. After compound dries, apply a second thin coat, feathering it out at the edges. Wait a day, then sponge, prime, and paint.

REPAIRING PANELING

1 When paneling has been punctured, burned, or otherwise seriously damaged, you must replace an entire 4x8-foot section. Using a putty knife and a pry bar, carefully remove baseboard and top molding. Pull nails with pliers. Any panels that are not butt-joined need to be cut before being removed to avoid damaging adjacent panels. Before cutting, consider what's behind the wall. Is your paneling fastened to studs or furring strips, or was it cemented to drywall or masonry? If the backing is solid, adjust your circular saw's cutting depth to avoid damaging the blade, or make cuts with a chisel. Mark lines about 3 inches in from panel edges and cut.

2 First, remove the center section of the panel you've cut. Begin pulling the section off the wall at the bottom, where there is usually no adhesive. Pull nails as they pop. When the center section is removed, you can get to the side pieces easily. Again, pry with care so you don't damage adjacent panels.

4 Refit the panel and secure by partially driving nails along the top. Pull panel 8 inches away from the wall at the bottom and prop it there until adhesive is tacky. Pull out the prop and press the panel to the wall. Fix it to adhesive by tapping the surface with a padded block.

3 Scrape old adhesive off studs, furring strips, or the wall with a scraper or cold chisel. Fit a new panel in place; remove it and apply a bead of panel adhesive as shown.

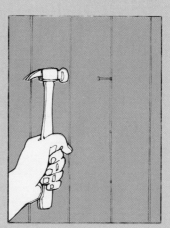

5 Sink nails in the grooves that have studs behind them and also along the top and bottom edges where they will be hidden by the molding.

REPAIRING CERAMIC TILE

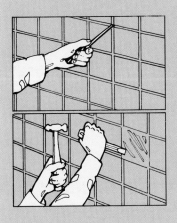

1 Take out the tiles you want to replace by chipping away the grout with a hammer and chisel. Smash the tiles one at a time and knock out the pieces. Scrape old adhesive from the wall.

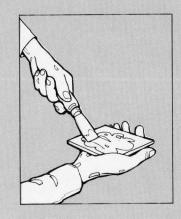

2 Use tile adhesive and a putty knife to butter the back of each new tile. Strive for a thin, even coat. Press a tile into place and center for grout spacing. Pound tile with your fist to fix the adhesive, then wipe off the excess immediately. Clean grout spaces and fill with grout.

SEALING AROUND A TUB

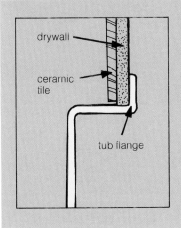

drywall

ceramic tile

tub flange

1 Bathtubs have their unseen ups and downs, caused by filling and emptying hundreds of pounds of water. Grout, a rigid mortar compound, can't withstand this flexing. The result: cracks where the tub meets the walls.

To fix them, first chip away the old grout between tub and walls.

2 Run an even bead of vinyl-base or silicone-base flexible caulking compound along the joint to fill the space. Caulk comes in smaller squeeze tubes as well as the cartridge container shown here.

To seal under a spout, unscrew it first. With faucets and showerheads, you usually need to remove only the decorative covers.

F inding an exact match is often one of the difficult parts of replacing damaged panels or tiles. If you're not lucky enough to have extra material saved from the original installation, you'll have to shop around. Bring home several samples and take time to find the right one. The neatest

repair job will still look makeshift if materials don't match.

Carefully removing the damaged panel or tile assures that you don't damage adjacent material. But don't expect to reuse anything you've taken

off the wall. Breakage is an inevitable part of removal.

These drawings show how to replace a single tile or panel, but the same techniques apply to replacing an entire wall surface. When you tile a large area, save time and effort by applying adhesive to the wall rather than to the tiles.

Caulk will fill any space where two materials meet. Vinyl and silicone types are best around bathtubs and other water sources. Apply caulk only to clean, dry surfaces.

WATERPROOFING BASEMENTS

Basement walls suffer from the same ills that plague the other walls in your house, and they have one special problem of their own: moisture. The difference between belowground tempera-ture (usually a constant 55 degrees Fahrenheit) and the air upstairs or outside often makes some basement mustiness inevitable.

If the walls sweat or if puddles of water collect on the floor, it's time to fight back. A wet basement wastes space, and it could undermine the footings and foundation walls of your home.

The chart below shows the four possible sources of be-lowground moisture problems. Simple tests help you uncover the culprits. In tracking down the water's origin, don't neglect the possibility that the moisture may be the result of a combination of these factors.

WHERE'S THE WATER COMING FROM?

PROBLEM	SYMPTOM/TEST	CAUSE	SOLUTION
CONDENSATION	Mold and mildew, damp walls, rusty metal, and dripping pipes. To test for condensation, tape a mirror in the dampest spot and wait 24 hours. If the mirror becomes foggy or beaded with water, suspect condensation.	The cause is moisture-laden air from an internal source (basement shower, washing machine, or unvented dryer) or a significant temperature difference between the walls and the inside air.	Improve ventilation, install a dehumidifier, or seal the interior walls.
SEEPAGE	Dampness on the floor or a particular wall, especially near floor level. As with condensation, tape a mirror to the wall. If moisture condenses behind it, seepage is the problem.	Surface water is forcing through pores in the foundation or wall-floor joint. Check roof drainage and window wells.	Improve surface drainage. If the problem is minor, an interior masonry sealer may work. If not, waterproof the foundation from the outside.
LEAKS	Small areas where water seems to be oozing or even trickling from a foundation wall or floor. Check the damp area carefully; note condition of mortar joints between blocks.	Cracks may be from normal settling, or an abnormal condition such as faulty roof drainage or improper surface grading.	A single hole may be plugged from inside with waterproof hydraulic cement. Or, you may have to work from outside by waterproofing the exterior surface and/or installing perimeter drain tiles.
UNDERGROUND WATER	A thin, hard-to-see film of water on the basement floor could be the first sign. Test by laying down vinyl sheet goods or plastic for two or three days. If moisture is penetrating, it will dampen the concrete underneath the barrier.	A spring or high water table is forcing water up from below, under high pressure in most cases. This may happen only in rainy periods.	Drain tiles installed around the perimeter of the foundation or floor might direct water to a lower spot or a storm sewer, or you may need a sump pump.

PLUGGING HOLES AND CRACKS

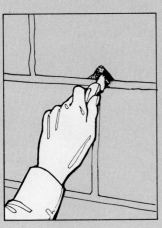

1 Slightly enlarge the hole with a cold chisel. Make the hole wider underneath than on the surface. This "keys" the plug so it can't pop loose. Clean out the hole with a dry brush and vacuum up residue.

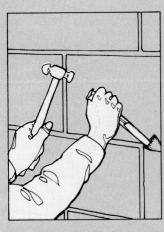

2 Mix plugging cement; use quick-hardening expansive cement or epoxy compound if water will be coming in under pressure while you're making the repair. Work it into a stopper shape with one end slightly larger than the diameter of the hole.

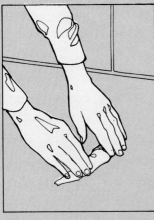

3 When the cement begins to stiffen, cork it into the hole and hold it in place for 3 to 4 minutes. Then smooth the surface with a trowel before the cement completely hardens. Check your plug from time to time. A new leak near your original plug may mean water is backing up against the foundation or under the floor.

4 Cracks need to be cut back to sound material. Bevel the edges of your cut so the crack is wider underneath.

5 Turn the mortar with a trowel several times, then pack it into the crack. Use the tip of the trowel to work the mix in well. Force the mix into the very back of the crack first, then fill the surface.

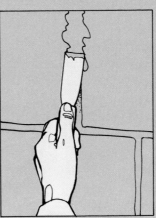

6 After the mortar begins to harden, pack it again, then shave off any excess with a wet trowel, pointing tool, or putty knife.

HOW TO READ
A BLUEPRINT

Architects use a special language of lines, symbols, and seemingly cryptic annotations on a sheaf of blue-gray papers known as *blueprints*. Chapter 6 introduces you to the fundamentals of drawing simple plans. Here's a more detailed guide to understanding what a professionally prepared blueprint can tell you.

There are minor variations according to different architects' preferences, but the fundamental characteristics of blueprints remain uniform throughout the building industry. This means that, with just a little help, you can make sense of the maze of lines that map a home from the conception of its design through the construction.

The house shown in the photograph *above* and simplified schematic drawing at *right*

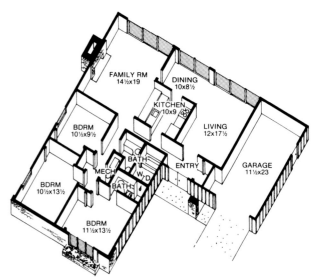

was built from blueprints partially represented by the drawings at *right*. Compare them to our schematic and you can visualize how the finished rooms will look.

Blueprints are usually drawn to "¼-inch scale"—¼ inch on the plan is equivalent to 1 foot of actual measurement. There are some exceptions to this system, but the *legend* that usually appears on the bottom of a blueprint always has a notation that indicates the scale.

Room sizes are frequently noted by numbers and arrows placed within the "room." Occasionally a scale line marked off in "feet" accompanies the drawings. With the aid of a compass, you can learn any dimension on the drawing.

A legend and/or a *finishing schedule* somewhere on one of the pages of plans shows the symbols used, including any special symbols used only by that architect. (Typical symbols are shown on page 155.) The finishing schedule also lists materials and special equipment to be used in the house.

Special notes

Additional help comes in the form of brief notations that are usually written near the point of reference, or footnoted by small arrows or symbols that refer you to a notation elsewhere. For example, examine the hearth in the family room blueprint shown at *upper right* and you'll discover that additional information can be learned by checking elevation No. 1.

Elevations are the final important components in a set of blueprints. The following page explains what you can learn from them.

(continued)

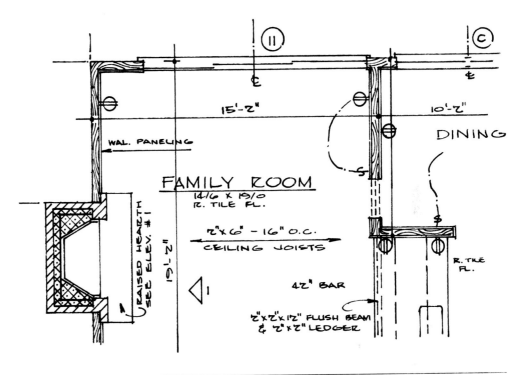

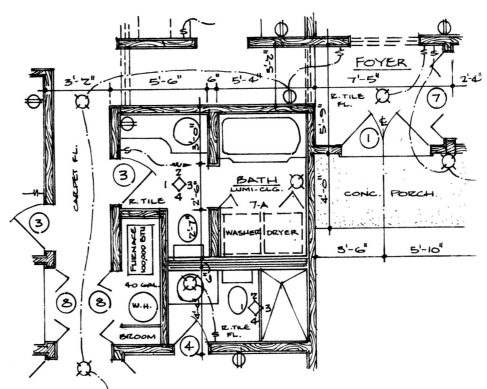

HOW TO READ
A BLUEPRINT
(continued)

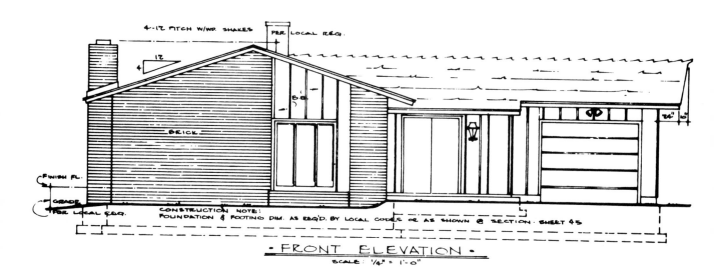

- FRONT ELEVATION -
SCALE: 1/4" = 1'-0"

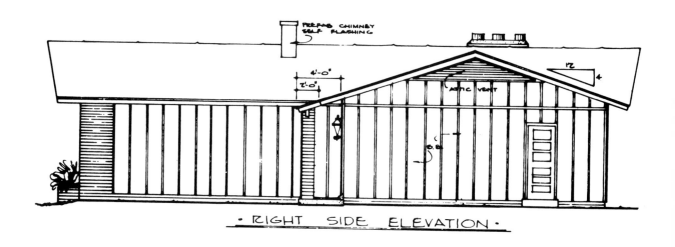

- RIGHT SIDE ELEVATION -

Couple *elevation* drawings with floor plans like the ones shown on the preceding page and you can visualize a house in three dimensions. Compare, for instance, the drawing at the top of this page with the photograph on page 152. Both show how the front of the house looks from head on.

The lower elevation view depicts it from the right side, and

additional drawings, not included here, show the rear and other side. Again, everything is drawn to exact scale, key measurements are indicated, and special information is noted. Typically, elevations also specify materials to be used.

Some—but not all—interior walls merit elevation drawings, too. Generally, if an architect or designer can describe how a wall is to be built with a few

simple notes on the floor plan, he or she will not bother to prepare an elevation view. But more complicated situations— a wall of built-ins, for instance, or an unusual arrangement of windows and doors—call for special instructions that are best communicated with a vertical depiction of what's to be done. Pages 96, 97, and 100

explain how to draw the simple elevations you might need for a wall or ceiling project.

Two other types of drawings sometimes included in blueprints are not shown here. A *section* shows how a house would look if part of it were sliced away. A *detail* provides a closeup look at an individual element that would be difficult or impossible to understand in ¼-inch scale.

Symbols shown on this page are used throughout blueprints. Space doesn't permit illustration of all symbols used, but if you understand the principles of these, you should have no trouble with others.

 Overhead or wall light. Unless otherwise marked, this means merely a socket for a light bulb. Lights in special fixtures such as coves or entirely lighted ceilings are specifically identified by type.

Double convenience outlet. This type of outlet allows for two electric plugs.

Hose bibb. This is simply a name for an outdoor connection for your garden hose.

SS₃ **Wall switch.** The small "3" beside the letter "s" indicates a three-way switch. The light operated by this switch also can be operated by another switch at the other end of the circuit. Dashes leading away from the switches show which lights or outlets are operated by that switch.

Telephone outlet. This does not mean that you will have a telephone in each of these locations. It means that the wire connection for a future phone is located at that point.

Power outlet. This usually is 220-volt. Do not confuse this with a double convenience outlet.

→A
→A **This symbol** means somewhere else on the plans you will find a vertical "cutaway" section drawing of this part of the house. The arrows point in the direction you would be looking toward.

〰 **Warm-air outlet.** This shows the location of the register.

 Dotted lines. These indicate something either behind what is shown or, on a plan, an object above what is shown. A plan is actually a horizontal section through a house, taken roughly 4 feet above the floor. For that reason, objects above the "line" are invisible and, therefore, "dotted."

 The swing of a door or casement window. Where no swing is shown for a window, the glass is fixed or the window is double-hung.

 Center line.

 Gas outlet.

O.C. **On centers.** Framing is measured from the center of one framing member to the center of the next—usually 16 inches.

W.C. **Water closet.** A toilet.

M.C. **Medicine cabinet.**

T&G **Tongue-and-groove.** Applies to sheathing, flooring, paneling.

G.I. **Galvanized iron.**

DS **Downspout.**

① **Numbered symbols** indicate the type of door to be used in each opening. Somewhere else in the plans you will find a *door schedule* that gives a small drawing or description of each door, with details on glass size, number of panels, and louvers.

Ⓑ **Lettered symbols** refer to the type of window in each opening. A *window schedule* elsewhere in the plans gives size, material, and number of panes in each window.

Building materials symbols are indicated on the floor plan or on a section drawing. The symbols following are frequently used on the floor plan to indicate the kind of materials used.

 Common brick.

 Concrete.

 Concrete block.

 Wood (stud walls).

 Structural glass.

Stone.

 A frame exterior wall—one made of studs with clapboards, shingles, or plywood as a face material—is measured from outside face of stud to outside face of stud. This is usually 1 to 2 inches from the outside wall surface.

 Masonry walls are dimensioned from the outside face of the wall.

 Brick veneer walls are measured from the face of the studs, like a frame wall. The distance from the stud facing to the outside face of the brick is dimensioned separately.

Interior partitions. The same general dimensioning rules hold true, with one exception. Stud partitions are dimensioned to the center line of the partition. All other types of partitions are dimensioned to the masonry face.

 Vertical dimensions are always measured from the *finished* floor line. Room heights are measured from the finished floor line to the plate line (framing member to which ceiling joists are fastened).

WHERE TO GO FOR MORE INFORMATION

Better Homes and Gardens® Books

Would you like to learn more about decorating, remodeling, or maintaining your walls and ceilings? These Better Homes and Gardens® books can help.

Better Homes and Gardens®
NEW DECORATING BOOK
How to translate ideas into workable solutions for every room in your home. Choosing a style, furniture arrangements, windows, walls and ceilings, floors, lighting, and accessories. 433 color photos, 76 how-to illustrations, 432 pages.

Better Homes and Gardens®
COMPLETE GUIDE TO HOME REPAIR,
MAINTENANCE, & IMPROVEMENT
Inside your home, outside your home, your home's systems, basics you should know. Anatomy and step-by-step drawings illustrate components, tools, techniques, and finishes. 515 how-to techniques, 75 charts, 2,734 illustrations, 552 pages.

Better Homes and Gardens®
COMPLETE GUIDE TO GARDENING
A comprehensive guide for beginners and experienced gardeners. Houseplants, lawns and landscaping, trees and shrubs, greenhouses, and insects and diseases. 461 color photos, 434 how-to illustrations, 37 charts, 552 pages.

Better Homes and Gardens®
STEP-BY-STEP
BASIC PLUMBING
Getting to know your system, solving plumbing problems, making plumbing improvements, and plumbing basics and procedures. 42 projects, 200 illustrations, 96 pages.

Better Homes and Gardens®
STEP-BY-STEP
BASIC WIRING
Getting to know your system, solving electrical problems, making electrical improvements, and electrical basics and procedures. 22 projects, 286 illustrations, 96 pages.

Better Homes and Gardens®
STEP-BY-STEP
BASIC CARPENTRY
Setting up shop, choosing tools and building materials, mastering construction techniques, building boxes, hanging shelves, framing walls, and installing drywall and paneling. 10 projects, 191 illustrations, 96 pages.

Better Homes and Gardens®
STEP-BY-STEP
MASONRY & CONCRETE
Choosing tools and materials; planning masonry projects; working with concrete; working with brick, block, and stone; and special-effect projects. 10 projects, 200 drawings, 96 pages.

Better Homes and Gardens®
STEP-BY-STEP
HOUSEHOLD REPAIRS
Basic tools for repair jobs; repairing walls and ceilings, floors and stairs, windows and doors, and electrical and plumbing items. 200 illustrations, 96 pages.

Better Homes and Gardens®
STEP-BY-STEP
CABINETS AND SHELVES
Materials and hardware, planning guidelines, the ABCs of cabinet construction, cutting and joining techniques, project potpourri. 155 illustrations, 96 pages.

Other Sources of Information

Most professional associations publish lists of their members, and will be happy to furnish these lists upon request. They also may offer educational material and other information.

American Hardboard Association (AHA)
887-B Wilmette Rd.
Palatine, IL 60067
Membership includes manufacturers representing major U.S. producers of hardboard.

ACKNOWLEDGMENTS

American Home Lighting Institute
230 N. Michigan Ave.
Chicago, IL 60601
Membership includes manufacturers, distributors, and retailers of residential lighting fixtures. The institute also trains lighting specialists.

Ceilings and Interior Systems Contractors Association (CISCA)
1800 Pickwick Ave.
Glenview, IL 60025
Membership includes ceilings and interior systems contractors. The association develops standards pertaining to workmanship, job conditions, and operating techniques. It also conducts sales training programs.

Cellulose Manufacturers Association (CMA)
5908 Columbia Pike
Baileys Crossroads, VA 22041
Membership includes manufacturers of cellulose insulation. The association educates the public about characteristics and uses of cellulose thermal insulation.

Exterior Insulation Manufacturers Association (EIMA)
1000 Vermont Ave. NW, Suite 1200
Washington, DC 20005
Membership includes manufacturers of exterior insulation wall and finish systems. The association acts as a sounding board for technical issues that need to be addressed.

Gypsum Association
1603 Orrington Ave.
Evanston, IL 60201
Membership includes miners and manufacturers of gypsum and gypsum products. The association sponsors basic and applied research programs at educational institutions and commercial testing laboratories on fire-resistant assemblies, wallboard application techniques, and new uses for gypsum products.

National Association of the Remodeling Industry (NARI)
11 E. 44th St.
New York, NY 10017
Membership includes contractors, manufacturers, wholesalers, lenders, utilities, and publishers. The association promotes the common business interests of the remodeling industry.

Tile Council of America
Box 326
Princeton, NJ 08540
Membership includes manufacturers of ceramic tile. Booklets are available on how best to use ceramic tile, as well as information on do-it-yourself tile installation.

Architects and Designers

Following is a page-by-page listing of the architects and designers whose work appears in this book.

Page 7
Sally Margoles
Page 9
Michael Vincent
Pages 12-13
Imperial Wallcoverings, a Collins & Aikman Co.
Pages 14-15
Judith Flamenbaum
Pages 16-17
Carol R. Knott
Pages 18-19
Richard Caldwell
Pages 20-21
Dale Anderson, Dale Carol Anderson Ltd.
Pages 24-25
Sherrye Henry
Pages 26-27
Adolfo Garcia
Pages 30-31
Z-Brick, Division of VMC Corp.
Page 32-33
Anthony Moses; Suzanne Brangham
Pages 34-35
Bob Allen
Pages 48-49
John Bloodgood
Pages 50-51
Stephen Mathias; James Miles
Pages 52-53
H. Anthony Smith, Arkhora Assoc., Inc.; photograph on page 53 courtesy of Shaker-town Corp.
Pages 62-63
J. David Doolin; Keith Gasser, Jesse Benesch & Assoc.
Pages 64-65
Suzy Taylor
Page 66
Z-Brick, Division of VMC Corp.
Pages 68-69
Pasquale Vazzana

Pages 74-75
Frederick Merrill, Jr.
Pages 76-77
Claire Cook, Casella Interiors
Pages 78-79
John H. Stone III, Louis Mazor Inc.; Pamela Bookey
Pages 80-81
Sara Giovanitti; Hilda Soloman & Assoc.
Pages 82-83
Robert E. Dittmer
Pages 84-85
Richard Freiwald; Nanci Cohen
Pages 86-87
Nancy Rolison; David Durant
Pages 88-89
Howard Atkinson
Pages 90-91
Gary Mahaffey
Pages 92-93
Mark Kaufman
Pages 120-121
Zoper and Slade
Pages 124-125
David Ashe
Pages 126-127
Joram Altman

Photographers and Illustrators

We extend our thanks to the following photographers and illustrators, whose creative talents and technical skills contributed much to this book.

Ross Chapple, Mike Dieter, George de Gennaro, Harry Hartman, Hedrich-Blessing, Bill Helms, William Hopkins & Assoc., Fred Lyon, Marine Arts, E. Alan McGee, Jordon Miller, Bradley Olman, Maris/Semel, Ozzie Sweet, Jessie Walker

Page numbers in *italics* refer to photographs or illustrated text.